KINGDOM HOLINESS

Louise,

Recently Gene Miller finished reading Kingdom Holiness and graciously offered to purchase some additional copies for me to sign and share with others. I have chosen several folks from Brighton Pres. who in small but significant ways, sowed into my early life of faith. This book is just some of that fruit. I pray you will be blessed and encouraged by it. Thank you.

Love in Christ,

Roger Woodworth

(Bill of course, would have been included in the sowing into my life).

KINGDOM HOLINESS

Holy Living in Our Challenging Culture

Rodger Woodworth

New Harbor Press

RAPID CITY, SD

Woodworth/New Harbor Press
1601 Mt.Rushmore Rd, Ste 3288
Rapid City, SD 57701
www.newharborpress.com

Kingdom Holiness/Rodger Woodworth. -- 1st ed.
ISBN 978-1-63357-202-7

CONTENTS

PRAISE FOR KINGDOM HOLINESS

"When Jesus explained the nature of true discipleship, the familiar practices of denying our neighbors, taking up our comforts, and following our dreams were absent from his vision. If we would follow him, we must instead deny ourselves, take up our crosses, and follow him. In the spirit of Bonhoeffer and through the lens of 2 Peter, Rodger Woodworth writes as both a teacher and a practitioner of true discipleship. I pray his words would lead you into a deeper holiness, and through it a deeper joy."
- Scott Sauls, senior pastor of Christ Presbyterian Church, Nashville TN, and author of several books, including Jesus Outside the Lines and Irresistible Faith

"Discipleship; real and biblically authentic discipleship, is hard. Rodger Woodworth has the experience of a seasoned disciple and the wisdom of a learned rabbi that combined makes his admonition in Kingdom Holiness a timely must read. If you want an easy life as a Christian put this book down, but if you are serious about living out your faith with integrity, then dig in and prepare to engage!"
- Rev Dr. D. Dean Weaver, Lead Pastor, Memorial Park Church, Pittsburgh PA.
Chaplain, Grove City College and Moderator of the Evangelical Presbyterian Church

"Rodger Woodworth's Kingdom Holiness isn't just a vanity-driven project of his conventional sermons but a true gift to those wanting guidance about how a gospel-centered Kingdom vision sends us into the world. Rodger not only has thought deeply about our world, but he has actually embodied God's holy principles in the gritty details of the beloved city in which he lives. In an era of experiencing modernity's pressures and deepening culture wars, the good news according to 2 Peter, in Dr. Woodworth's hands, comes alive as a lifeline. Read this book and be encouraged to actually live "in but not of" our secular age, in real Kingdom holiness."

- Byron Borger, owner of Hearts & Minds Bookstore, Dallastown, PA.

"Rodger Woodworth has been thinking: thinking deeply about the kingdom of God and our particular moment, the church and its readiness to engage in God's mission. He has also been reading across an unusually broad and diverse set of sources. The result is a book that is at once strongly challenging and strangely encouraging. I cannot recommend it highly enough."

- Dan Dupee, Chairman, Coalition for Christian Outreach, Pittsburgh, PA.

"Rarely do you find the powerful blend of orthodoxy & orthopraxy in one person. Rev. Dr. Rodger Woodworth brings a unique perspective to holiness in our changing 21st century culture of age, gender, ethnicity and economic diversity."

- Rufus Smith, Sr. Pastor, Hope Church, Memphis, TN.

ACKNOWLEDGEMENTS

I am married to Wende, my college sweetheart, I am the father of two, and a grandfather of nine. I was the founding pastor of interracial churches in the North Side of Pittsburgh and in downtown Pittsburgh. Along with being the Director of Cross Cultural Ministries for the Coalition for Christian Outreach, I was also an adjunct seminary professor at Reformed Presbyterian Theological Seminary. I am presently teaching at an Anglican seminary called Trinity School for Ministry. I have a Doctorate of Ministry in Complex Urban Settings and served on the Board of Directors for several local ministries. My greatest passion, however, is for the gospel of grace that saves broken people like me and broken people different than me and makes us all equal at the foot of the cross.

It was in the midst of such a broken community of mutuality, both inside and outside the church, that I learned that God purifies our faith best in the hard realities of every day life in this world. Yet, like many of us, I longed for a more comfortable Christian walk, separated from the world, where my expectations are fulfilled, and I can avoid the heartaches and hardships that a sovereign God often allows and even orchestrates. Nearly forty years of life and ministry in the city, however, had revealed to me that I was desiring a one-sided theology that often resisted anything that felt like crucifixion of my pleasurable life. Ironically, in the end I was left with a joyless experience of God's Kingdom. It was only as I learned to hear and embrace both the praises and the laments, in my life and in the life of others, that I began to discover the shalom of God's Kingdom - that place of tension where I no longer "copy the behavior and customs of this world but let God transform me into a new person" (Romans 12:2). It was there that I began to understand I was learning and growing more in my faith, through the trials of life rather than the comforts of life. It is my belief and experience that the American church has chosen a similar role of comfort in our challenging culture. Instead of a loving and gracious cultural engagement, we have settled down in our respective theological foxholes to manage and maintain what we have, in order to keep from losing any more ground to the unbelieving world.

This book was formed out of a sermon series on 2 Peter that I preached in the winter of 2015. I have added insights from the seminary classes I teach on mission and church planting, along with thoughts from my doctoral dissertation entitled, *Developing an Urban Discipleship for the Suburban Church*. I also gained much wisdom and direction from studying the following commentaries:

- *The NIV Application Commentary on 2 Peter, Jude* by Douglas Moo
- *The Message of 2 Peter & Jude, The Bible Speaks Today* by Lucas and Green
- *The IVP New Testament Commentary Series, 2 Peter & Jude* by Harvey and Towner
- *Expository Sermons on 2 Peter* by D.M. Lloyd Jones
- *2 Peter & Jude: An Introduction and Commentary* by Michael Green
- *Hebrews; 1 and 2 Peter, Calvin's New Testament Commentaries, Vol. 12*

I owe a deep gratitude to my wife, my family and some dear friends, who strongly encouraged me to sit down and finally write my first book. Thank you to the members of the communities where I had the honor to plant and pastor churches; I learned so much from you. I pray this book challenges and encourages Christ's church.

"We're too comfortable to be spiritual ... we think we will be able to pursue God better without danger or hardship. And yet it works in just the opposite way. Nothing is more difficult to grow spiritually when comfortable." Tim Bascom, *The Comfort Trap: Spiritual Dangers in the Convenience Culture* (Intervarsity, 1993).

INTRODUCTION

A young boy carried the cocoon of a moth into his house to watch the fascinating events that would take place when the womb emerged. When the moth finally started to break out of his cocoon, the boy noticed how very hard the moth had to struggle. The process was very slow. In an effort to help, he reached down and widened the opening of the cocoon. Soon the moth was out of its prison. But as the boy watched, the wings remained shriveled. Something was wrong. What the boy had not realized was that the struggle to get out of the cocoon was essential for the moth's muscle system to develop. In a misguided effort to relieve a struggle, the boy had crippled the future of this creature. Not unlike the moth, the trials of life in this world, are necessary for our spiritual growth and the development of God's Kingdom.

God not only understands this but He has designed and allowed the struggles of our lives to purify our faith. Many of those struggles today come in the form of our challenging culture that rejects and often opposes the Christian faith. Jesus prayed to His heavenly Father not to take us out of this world because just as God sent Jesus into the world, Jesus was sending us into the world (John 17:15,17). It is one of several Scriptures where we get the saying, "we are to be in the world but not of the world." This means, as the church, we have two callings. We are called to a certain worldliness, having been sent into the world to get involved in the life of the culture around us. We are also called to be holy because God is holy (Leviticus 19:2), "But now you must be holy in everything you do, just as God who chose you is holy" (1 Peter 1:15).

This dual calling doesn't allow us to be holy by escaping the world, nor surrender our holiness by conforming to the world. We are called to a kind of "kingdom holiness." [1] What I mean by a "kingdom holiness" is not adapting to a Christian culture around us that is more or less holy, but rather fully engaging an unholy culture while conforming to the character of God as a citizen of His Kingdom. This constant tension and balancing between a commitment to holy living and our challenging culture becomes the very trial laden method of God's discipleship. This is why the Apostle Peter exhorts his readers to "greatly rejoice" in their trials because our purified faith is more precious than gold (1 Peter 1:6). There is no trial free life, no one makes it through this life without experiencing God's purposeful tests. J.I. Packer wrote, "It needs to be said loud and clear that in the Kingdom of God there ain't no comfort zone and never will be." [2]

Yet as George Barna discovered, the most appealing methods of discipleship are "those that are least intrusive, emotionally and personally." [3] Our sinful nature desires "protective buffers" from any growth process found in the harsh realities of our world. Consequently churches have developed methodologies that are more focused on membership than maturity and on management than mission. While these tools are not morally wrong they introduce a human dynamic that produces only human results - results that can lead people to pursue goals that are inconsistent with the values and holy life of God's Kingdom. Simple cause and effect methods have led us to assume that increasing attendance will lead to a holy life. If it is bigger it must be better. The church, to its credit, has found unique and relevant paradigms to get people to cross the barriers to attending church, but getting occasional church attenders to become committed followers of Christ remains a challenge. People have often become Christians for the benefits they find in Christ: help for a marriage, family programs and of course the promise of heaven. It is possible that the commitment barrier has become so formidable the church has settled for having comfortable attenders. However, it also creates what Dr. Doug

Hall calls a "soft reality ... a less harsh world that coddles and shelters us from a level of learning." [4] In other words it creates a learning disability. It is actually in the hard social realities of life that we become in tune with what God is doing in the world around us, and the world around us wants Christianity out of the way so life can continue on its comfortable vacation cruise. Like a chaplain on a cruise ship, we are only needed for a token prayer if the ship encounters a serious storm "but not taken very seriously when the weather is fine." [5]

Many in the church have gone along with this assessment that Christianity no longer has any thing distinctive to offer. Rodney Clapp refers to this as "sentimental capitulation" and points to one proponent who claims, "The only genuine way to 'interact with the emerging world' is to concede most of the game to it." [6] There is literally no discipleship option needed here because we are just along for the ride and to offer a ceremonial role at weddings and funerals.

Another response to Christianity being shoved to the sidelines is what Clapp calls "retrenchment." He sees two forms of this; the first is a remnant of the religious right who desire to "act as a chaplain that has gained some of the power the chaplaincy held in earlier Christendom." [7] There is a resurgence of a Christian nationalism today that fits into this retrenchment. The second and most popular retrenchment, however, is the idea "that Christianity is really about making people healthy and wealthy" and "is a necessary component in the successful pursuit of happiness." [8] Clapp continues,

> Therapeutic and marketing techniques are key for these retrenchers. They read McDonald's ads more carefully than they do the Bible, then declare, 'You deserve a break today. And the whole purpose of God's existence is to give it to you.' What they present are...the Be-Happy Attitudes . . . They are not stances that question the dominant culture; instead they embody it. [9]

Advertising and marketing tap into our most basic human desires for sex, money and power, the historic and unholy trinity of our world. When Christianity unwittingly adopts this message, it only plays into our sinful nature that desires comfort and convenience while being insulated from any intrusion of those hard realities in life. We end up with a church that believes like theists but live like atheists. Our profession and practice, our belief and behavior, do not line up.

Reinforcing this retrenchment are the many "isms" that surround us today offering to numb and buffer us from anything that would disturb our happiness. To be comfortable, life must be practical (pragmatism) and pleasurable (hedonism with a moral acceptability). In order for life to be practical and pleasurable we need the philosophy of materialism – being more concerned with material than spiritual values. Joseph Stowell says, "The real point of materialism is not how much we have, but what has us. The test of materialism is whether our goods have made us... self-sufficient or God-sufficient." [10]

One final philosophy of our world that may be the foundation for the other three is individualism – where we lead our own life, in our own way, without regard for others. This is a philosophy that states, "I am a free agent, I am independent and I am my own person." Eugene Peterson writes, "There can be no maturity in the spiritual life, no obedience in following Jesus, no wholeness in the Christian life, apart from an immersion in, and embrace of, community. I am not myself by myself." [11]

Individualism contradicts Paul who says, "Now all of you together are Christ's body and each one of you is a separate and necessary part of it" (1 Corinthians 12:27). However, the predominant world system "focuses not on community but on the individual, interpreted as a maximizer of self-interest . . . whatever good or goal someone lives for is accordingly a 'private' and never a 'public' matter." [12] Individualism with its accompanying "isms" seeks a less harsh world, a softer reality, but the result is a diminished learning process. We are left without the negative feedback that can begin to tell us how God is at work and whether we are headed in the right direction or not.

As Christians continue to be co-opted by the prevailing culture, a church consumerism has created a migration pattern that chases whatever church has the newest and biggest programs. While every church suffers under consumerism, rural and urban churches have deeper cultural and family ties that limit the church mobility seen in the suburbs. It is in the more affluent neighborhoods, where the covert pressure is to move upward in housing and jobs and where children labeled as gifted are nurtured toward success. It is also where Christians seek self-interest through leaving the disillusionment of one church for the greener pastures of another. The perception that a church is no longer meeting one's spiritual or felt needs is, in most cases, narcissistic and driven by the arrogance of individualism. David Goetz, an editor for Leadership magazine, writes,

> Frustration and conflict are the raw materials of spiritual development. All the popular reasons given for shopping for another church are actually spiritual reasons for staying put. They are a means of grace, preventing talk of spirituality from becoming sentimental or philosophical. Biblical spirituality is earthy, face-to-face, and often messy. [13]

Spiritual growth, into holy living, does not happen without a long-term commitment to a neighborhood church with all its imperfections, where people different than us can sand off our rough edges. The problem is most people are more than willing to be the sandpaper but few are willing to be sanded. It is the conflicts, disappointments and hurts experienced in the church and the community, that can provide an opportunity for growth. The spiritual life cannot always be tamed, it must remain a frontier rather than made suburban. Goetz, who lives in suburbia and defines it as cozy, safe, homogeneous and affluent, says, "So much of suburban life seems to be about preventing the tornado." [14] The entire physical organization of suburbia is set up to create comfort and condition behavior and what is true sociologically may be true spiritually. Goetz agrees and states, "It's not that suburbanites don't suffer as much as rural or city folks, but perhaps we struggle more to deny suffering's reality. And sometimes we have to go out of our way to have it revealed. One way to confront this denial is as old as the Christian faith: voluntarily entering into the suffering of others." [15]

He goes on to write about a friend who volunteers at a homeless shelter. The friend admits that he is still not very good at entering into the suffering of others but since his life is so sheltered with material blessings, at least he is forced to think about the sufferings of others.

Regardless of where one lives, David Goetz seems to understand that a comfortable spirituality may not be an asset when it comes to discipleship and spiritual growth but rather a soft reality that coddles and protects us, creates a hindrance to learning. It is true sociologically and theologically. Blacks in our previous church overcame their history of racism and discrimination by whites, to accept me as their white pastor. That experience continues to transform me. As I watched the poor in our church, I grew into a deeper understanding of "the poor are rich in faith" (James 2:5), and what it meant to "be content in all circumstances" (Philippians 4:12). It has removed ingratitude in me towards God on more than one occasion. Author Amy Sherman wrote, "Seeing the needs firsthand softens our heart and makes them break for the things that break God's heart." [16] Both history and Scripture reveal that when we engage suffering and hardships, whether in the lives, or the internal strife, of a diverse church, or an outreach into our challenging culture, there is God's hand of discipleship and in embracing it we begin a transformational journey into a holy life.

It is this engagement with today's challenging culture that is God's most prominent method for developing committed Christians. In

Center Church, Tim Keller writes, "The world that Christians in the West had known - where the culture titled in the direction of traditional Christianity - no longer existed. The culture had become a problem the church could no longer ignore." [17] When I was a teenager in the sixties, it was not unusual for a bank to request, from a loan applicant, a recommendation from their pastor, priest or rabbi. The bank not only wanted to know that the person had the financial ability to repay the loan but also the good character to pay it on time. To not go along with this cultural mindset was to be considered a nonconformist, a dissenter, and it may have prevented them from getting their loan approved. It was considered a general public fact that if you wanted to be seen as a good citizen in the place you lived, you would at least be associated with a church or synagogue.

In Lesslie Newbigin's lengthy article "Can the West Be Converted?", he unpacks a book by Peter Berger called *The Heretical Imperative*. In it he describes what Berger calls a plausibility structure. "A social structure of ideas and practices, which creates the conditions which determine whether or not a belief is plausible. To hold beliefs which fall outside this plausibility structure is to be a heretic (a nonconformist, a dissenter). It is just how things are and always have been." [18]

Some sixty years ago the plausibility structure allowed a bank, if it wanted, to ask you for a recommendation from a pastor. By contrast in today's post Christian culture, there is no one acceptable worldview, no one meta narrative, rather we construct our own stories. Many of the patterns of belief and behavior, which once guided our lives, and were rarely questioned, no longer exist. As a result, it is only reasonable that religion has also become a construct of our own personal narrative. It's an ongoing project of creating a comfortable faith environment, even at the risk of unraveling truth.

Newbigin goes on to write that human affairs have been divided into two realms - "the private and the public; a private realm of values where pluralism reigns and a public world of what our culture calls 'facts'." [19] Pluralism is where we are free to hold values and beliefs without judgment - at least theoretically. In our own private enclave, Christianity is allowed to believe and practice its particular world-view. Other world views have the same freedom and opportunity to live according to their version of reality. When any of these various perspectives of our existence comes in conflict Newbigin says, "we argue, we experiment, we carry out tests until we reach agreement about what are the facts, and then we expect all reasonable people to accept them. The one who does not accept them is the real heretic." [20]

Now this does not end in anyone being burnt at the stake, mainly because these accepted public facts are devoid of any values of good or bad. Facts are just facts and they are value free, but as such are highly regarded in our culture today. Facts are not concerned with purpose only cause and effect; how things work. If facts have no purpose there is no reason to be concerned whether it is good or bad, it just is. But if something has a purpose one can begin to determine its value based on whether it accomplishes that purpose. Newbigin quotes Alasdair MacIntyre to give an example from his book *After Virtue* with this factual statement,

> This watch has not lost five seconds in two years. This is a good watch, provided that watch is already under-stood as an instrument for keeping time. If 'watch' means only a collection of bits of metals which can be used according to the personal preference of its owner, for decorating the sitting room or throwing at the cat, than no such conclusion follows and everyone is free to have his or her own opinion as to whether it is a good watch or not [21]

This public realm of accepted facts has become the new plausibility structure, the prevailing worldview, where Christianity is now seen as the heretic, the nonconforming dissenter. For example the

Westminster Confession's chief end of man, to glorify God and enjoy Him forever, is now relegated to the private realm of church, not the public realm of facts and gay marriage and theories of evolution are considered value free, purposeless but accepted facts, leaving most of life without any significant meaning.

I agree with Newbigin who wrote, "It would be easy at this point to throw in some remarks about the disintegration which our culture is showing." [22] Instead, as he suggests, let's start asking the question "what does it mean for how we engage this culture", this public realm of facts that contradict the gospel. Newbigin asks,

> What would it mean if instead of trying to understand the gospel from the point of view of the culture, we tried to understand the culture from the point of view of the gospel. It will no longer do to accept the dichotomy between a public world of so called facts and a private world of so called values. We will have to be bold enough to confront our public world with the reality of Jesus Christ. I confess that when I say these things ... I can hardly imagine all that will entail. [23]

Here then is God's call to a kingdom holiness in this challenging culture. We can no longer be content that Christianity is at least one of many foxholes of truth among the ideology of pluralism. Just like the early church, we will need to face the challenges of the world's politics, economics and science, that believe no one can really know the truth. We must integrate the Christian faith into all of life so that a new realm can be discovered; that of God's coming Kingdom. And we must do that through the mission of God as it is carried out by His church, with all the grace and truth of Jesus our King. To this end Michael Frost asks, "What if we looked at the church's mission as empowering followers of Christ to infiltrate all the domains of society as agents of the mission of God?" [24] The public realm of facts needs to see this other option of reality.

Jesus tells two very short parables in Matthew 13:44-46. One is about a field hand, the other about a merchant. The first is probably a peasant working for a wealthy landowner and while plowing the field he turns up a box of coins. Evidently it was not unusual for people to bury their treasures and forget about them. So the field hand sells everything he has in order to buy the field containing the valuable coins. The discovery of the valuable coins causes his actions. The merchant is probably a man of more significant wealth as he is in the business of buying pearls – an extremely valuable commodity in those days. But he too invests everything he has in order to possess these pearls of great price and his discovery, likewise, causes his actions. Jesus says that both the coins and the pearls are like the Kingdom of Heaven and the discovery of it caused the men to act. They were literally carried away by their joy. Commentator Frederick Dale Bruner says, "The point, expanded, is this: joy is the engine of change." [25] Bruner goes on to say that selling was not a sacrifice it was a wise investment because of the value of the discovery. The discovery changed the lives of the peasant field hand and the wealthy merchant forever, having sold everything to buy the new reality. This is the option the public realm of facts needs to discover.

Paul says in Colossians 2:3 that in Jesus "lie hidden all the treasures of wisdom and knowledge". The hidden treasure of God's Kingdom discovered in the person and work of Jesus Christ moves people to make life-changing decisions motivated by the joy of the discovery. The joy keeps it from feeling like a sacrifice. Neither the field hand nor the merchant was told to do anything, the treasure tells it all. The discovery of God's Kingdom brings joyous responses not joyless duties. Joy enables selling but only selling gets the treasure, first the discovery, then the joy and then the selling to possess the treasure. In other words divine grace causes our human response and that divine grace can be seen in the truth of God's advancing Kingdom.

Oh that it would be that simple. In this public realm of accepted facts and the private world of pluralism, where truth is relativized, we are inundated with various versions of truth that all promise to make sense of the world in which we live. In our desire for comfort and in our lackadaisical attitude towards holy living, we are, sometimes, all too eager to listen. It is easier to presume on God's grace and settle for just being saved. In addition to our self-satisfied faith, our secular neighbors are no longer looking for that God-shaped void in their life. According to James K. A. Smith's exposition on Charles Taylor's commentary of our postmodern culture, "They don't have any sense that the 'secular' lives they have constructed are missing a second floor." [26] They have found enough significance, out of the world they have engineered, that they are not concerned with questions of God. This is what makes our culture so challenging and God's call to a kingdom holiness so important, because as Smith says, "The secular touches everything. It not only makes unbelief possible; it also changes belief - it impinges upon Christianity". [27] Is it possible that our comfortable Christian lifestyle is based in part on a defective doctrine digested from the secular world we live in? Have we settled into a comfortable syncretism of theological and ideological views that have left us with a diminished and powerless gospel? Are we left with a gospel that no longer reveals the Kingdom of God and the resulting joy that becomes the engine of change?

The Apostle Peter wrote his second letter to address such questions. He writes to address a complacency and false teaching that had infiltrated the church. His answer was to embrace the nonnegotiable truth of the Christian faith and to grow in that faith, as well as give a warning over his concerns about the influence of the false teachers. His letter doesn't make it clear whether the false teaching had contributed to the readers' comfortable faith or their faith had made them susceptible to an unbiblical doctrine. In reality it was probably both. In either case, what Peter was addressing was not so much the actual teaching but the way the teachers were living. Their libertine lifestyle was communicating that the grace of God allowed them, even as Christians, to do anything they desired. This was the "cheap grace" of Dietrich Bonhoeffer and consistent with Voltaire's excuse for sin - "God will forgive, that's his business".

Our challenging culture makes us just as susceptible to this false teaching today because of its deep suspicion, to outright rejection, of absolute truth. The various versions of truth found in our private pluralism and accepted public facts results in an individualized life-style of "whatever works for you". This pragmatism has caused many Christians to concede the dialogue, over truth, to the prevailing culture. We have become more comfortable with the practicality of what works than affirming the truth.

According to some, G. K. Chesterton wrote that "when people stop believing in God, they do not believe in nothing; they believe in any-thing." [28] The result is not skepticism but gullibility. When you are not feeling well we can choose from a variety of over the counter medications. In a similar way we can choose from a supermarket full of worldviews to help us understand our lives. Today in this marketplace of ideas, monopolies cannot be allowed, otherwise conflict will erupt. The only truth seems to be that tolerance must always override any other exclusive truth claims.

People fear the tyranny of a truth that says, "I must be obeyed" and yet tolerance leaves us with a permanent uncertainty. How then do we come together from these divergent sides of truth and tolerance? How do we engage this challenging culture today while maintaining the holy character of God? The Apostle Paul wrote that we "must not quarrel but must be kind to everyone.... we must teach effectively and be patient with difficult people" (2 Timothy 2:24). Jesus told Pilate, "I came to bring truth to the world" (John 18:37). However, He didn't stand for truth with a sword in His hand but rather a cross on His back. If we are going to reconcile truth and tolerance we must do it with Jesus' humility and compassion. If we are going to engage this chal-lenging culture, not in a war, but with the joy of God's Kingdom, we will need to get out of our foxholes to love those who oppose us. C. S. Lewis wrote, "I didn't go to religion to make me happy. I always knew a bottle of Port would do that. If you want a religion to make you feel really comfortable, I certainly don't recommend Christianity." [29]

This journey forward is rarely comfortable, while upholding the truth of the gospel and living out the character of Christ in the public realm of opposing facts. Yet it is in this tension between a kingdom holiness and our challenging culture that God will use to transform us and reveal more of His Kingdom by removing the impurities in our church and in our life. As you read, pray and marinate in this simple exposition of Peter's second letter, "May God bless you with his special favor and wonderful peace as you come to know Jesus, our God and Lord, better and better" (2 Peter 1:2). May we also move from a comfortable life to a more godly one.

PART 1 - THE TRUTH OF THE GOSPEL

"If you center your life and identity on pleasure, gratification, and comfort, you will find yourself getting addicted to something. You will become chained to the 'escape strategies' by which you avoid the hardness of life." Tim Keller, *The Reason for God.*

CHAPTER 1 - A COMFORTABLE LIFE OR A GODLY LIFE?

Warnings come in a lot of different forms. We smell smoke, hear an alarm, read a health report or see a weather forecast. And the responses to warnings vary. How eminent is the danger? How reliable is the source? Is it the forecast of a far off storm or the horn of a speeding car coming at you? Is the warning from a trusted friend or a passing stranger? The Apostle Peter's second letter is a warning, but it comes with instructions and hope and it will be up to the reader to decide how eminent is the danger and how reliable is the source.

Peter's second letter is concerned that the church had become stagnant and complacent, refusing to grow in their faith. He contributes much of this to teachers who were twisting the truth, a seductive influence that was destabilizing faithful believers and offering a more comfortable Christian experience. Peter's purpose, therefore, was to expose these false teachers but more importantly to reinforce the foundational truths of the gospel. His message is best summarized in the final two verses of his letter. "You already know these things, dear friends. So be on guard; then you will not be carried away by the errors of these wicked people and lose your own secure footing. Rather, you must grow in the grace and knowledge of our Lord and Savior Jesus Christ" (2 Peter 3:17-18).

So with his concerns in mind, Peter starts this letter, in verse 3, talking about the power of Christ that gives us everything we need to live a godly life. Not a comfortable life, nor a successful life, nor a prosperous life, but Jesus' divine power gives us everything we need to live a godly life. This tells us that there is no worry or temptation, not even our challenging culture, that we can't overcome because of Christ's power.

Do you ever wonder whether Jesus Christ is sufficient for your life? After all God has set some pretty high standards. "You must be holy because I am holy," God says (1 Peter 1:16). Yet Peter is telling us Jesus gives us the resources to meet those standards, even when life is hard. But how can we be sure we are meeting those standards?

In the rural home I grew up in, my father heated the main living area with an old potbelly stove. We had a traditional oil furnace, but to save money my dad preferred to cut wood and keep that old stove burning as the main source of heat. I loved coming home to visit in the winter because as we drove up our road I could tell whether dad had the stove fired up by the smoke coming out of the chimney and as we got closer, by the smell of the wood burning. Now I could see the smoke and could smell the wood but I could only imagine the scene in the living room. My dad opening the door to the stove and throwing another log on the fire. I could not see the internal work of my dad starting and stoking the fire. I could only see the outward evidence in the smoke coming out of the chimney.

So how do we know that Christ is sufficient for our lives, how do we know the power of Christ gives us everything we need to live a godly life? We can tell by the outward evidence of our good works (James 2:17) and by the fruit of the Spirit: love, joy peace, patience, kindness and the like (Galatians 5:22). If there is no smoke coming out of the chimney, there is no fire in the stove. If there is no semblance of godly activity coming out of our life, there is no power of

Christ in our soul. Only God the Father, working through Christ the Son, can provide the stove and the wood and only the Holy Spirit can start the fire that produces the evidence of a godly life. Peter is saying all the ingredients of grace needed for the evidence of this kind of life are provided in the power of Christ. Jesus as Lord of our lives sets the standards for living a godly life. But the good news is, as the author of our lives, Jesus also meets those standards by giving us the power to show evidence of a godly life. And here's the thing: part of that evidence is recognizing that when our life is not godly, we humbly come to God, asking for forgiveness. Jesus sets the standards for a godly life, a life that is not a perfect life, but rather it is a life of repentance and forgiveness. In Mathew 5:20 the disciple writes, "But I warn you—unless your righteousness is better than the righteousness of the teachers of religious law and the Pharisees, you will never enter the Kingdom of Heaven!"

The godly life, the smoke coming out of the chimney, must exceed the teachers of the law and the Pharisees. That's some serious evidence Jesus is requiring; that's some godly life, because the people who heard this from Jesus assumed the teachers and the Pharisees were models of perfection. Even though later Jesus would reveal that the Pharisees' perfection fell short because it was based on reconstructing the law so as to demand little from themselves, while demanding much from the people. However, Jesus taught that the law demanded the most from everyone. His demand was a God honoring life, a standard no one could meet. That's the whole point of the Sermon on the Mount. Jesus' teaching in chapters five, six and seven of Matthew's gospel, gives us the standard for living a life pleasing to God, a life that would exemplify living in the Kingdom of God. A godly life is not just, don't murder, but it's don't call your brother an idiot, it's not just, don't commit adultery, it's don't even lust in your heart. The standard for godly living is not just, love your neighbor, it's love your enemy. These are seemingly unattainable standards.

These are not even standards a few moralistic fanatics can meet. Yet these are the standards required to live in God's Kingdom.

The standards are so high, Christianity has hinted at lowering them so more people can reach them. Jerry Bridges, in his book *Pursuit of Holiness*, uses the term "cruise control obedience." [30] By that he means Christians who practice an obedience, at a certain level or speed, until they reach a perceived standard acceptable to others around them. Don't lie, but who can possibly keep from gossiping. Don't steal, but everybody fudges on their taxes. Abstain from sex outside of marriage between one man and one woman, but if you really love someone what's the harm. So we begin to subtly redefine a godly life. We will discover that's what Peter was concerned with. There were teachers redefining and changing the standards, twisting the truth, enabling people to become comfortable and complacent about living a godly life.

The word godly here is "eusebeia" in the Greek and it literally means good worship. It is a rare word in the New Testament but it is used to summarize the expected behavior of Christians who have come to know the God of Scripture. It is sometimes translated piety. [31] It is living a life that is perfectly pleasing to God. However, when challenged with this standard of godly living, it is easy to give in to despair and then settle for our own self-satisfied, comfortable, standard of a holy life.

So Jesus sets the requirements for godly living but again the good news is Jesus meets those standards for us. We don't have to water down God's expectation or lower the standards for a godly life. Jesus has given us everything we need to meet His standards. Some translations have the word "bestowed" because the Greek word has the idea of a royal or imperial gift. It's a word that abounds with generosity from a higher authority. Jesus Christ has generously "bestowed" all that could ever be needed to be godly, including his life's blood to cover our ungodly life. Just by being a Christian we have every thing we need.

During Super-bowl XXXVII, FedEx ran a commercial that spoofed the movie *Castaway*, in which Tom Hanks played a FedEx worker whose company plane went down, stranding him on a desert island for years. Looking like the bedraggled Hanks in the movie, the FedEx employee in the commercial goes up to the door of a suburban home, package in hand. When the lady comes to the door, he explains that he survived five years on a deserted island, and during that whole time he kept this package in order to deliver it to her. She gives a simple, "Thank you." But he is curious about what is in the package that he has been protecting for years. He says, "If I may ask, what was in that package after all?" She opens it and shows him the contents, saying, "Oh, nothing really. Just a satellite telephone, a global positioning device, a compass, a water purifier, and some seeds." Like the contents in this package, the resources for growing a godly life are available for every saved by grace Christian who will take advantage of them.

This comes with both a great encouragement and a great warning. It's an encouragement because it means there is nothing we need. The gospel is sufficient for us to meet God's requirements. Our trust in the efficacious work of Christ on the cross provides all we need. In other words, if there is something the word of God does not address, some moral, philosophical, scientific, or even personal question, we must assume it is not relevant to living a godly life. An unanswered question about dinosaurs does not diminish what Jesus provides to live a life that is pleasing to His Father. No matter how intriguing the mysteries of life may be from a human perspective, not having the answers does not keep us from a godly life.

Living a God honoring life does not come from Christ plus something else: healing, success, prosperity, or some special experience. Simply by being a Christian we have access to every thing we need to live a life pleasing to God. The sufficiency of Christ is the good news. Christ has deposited his right way of living into the checking account of our lives so we can never bounce a check with our sinful life. We always have enough of Christ's righteousness to come to him and ask for the grace of forgiveness.

But this sufficiency of Christ also comes with a warning because we have to face up to our responsibility to God. If Christ's power has given us everything we need we can't blame God for our not living a godly life. A godly life is not something only rich Christians can obtain or well- educated Christians or super spiritual Christians or only poor Christians. A godly life is within the reach of every Christian regardless of their lot in life. There is no secret sanctification process, no special experiential journey that we need to live a god honoring life. Christ's death and resurrection is sufficient to save and sufficient to make us holy. So if we are not living a godly life there is only one person to blame. It's not God, nor is it that woman he gave you, nor the man he gave you, it's not your friend or your neighbor, not even your enemy is to blame. It's because we've given up, given in, compromised or conceded, stagnated or staggered in our faith.

So, these questions remain: what is this power of Christ and how do we access it? How does Jesus enable us to meet his standards for living a godly life? Peter says, "By knowing Jesus better!" This is not just some facts about Jesus but knowing Jesus intimately and having an informed relationship that is a product of our conversion to the Gospel. Our knowledge of Christ increases our access to the power of Christ. And the power of Christ is the power of the Holy Spirit, our new Emanuel, God with us, the resource Christ provides to meet his standards of a holy life. In John 14:16-17, 26, the Apostle writes in his gospel,

> And I will ask the Father, and he will give you another Advocate, who will never leave you. He is the Holy Spirit, who leads into all truth. The world cannot receive him, because it isn't looking for him and doesn't recognize him. But you know him, because he lives with you now and later will be in you. But when

the Father sends the Advocate as my representative,
that is, the Holy Spirit, he will teach you everything
and will remind you of everything I have told you.

On the role and relationship of the Trinity, John Calvin wrote, "To
the Father is attributed the beginning of all activity, fountain and well-
spring of all things, (he is the initiator). To the Son, wisdom, counsel,
and the ordered disposition of all things, (he is the executor), but to
the Spirit is assigned the power and efficacy of that activity." [32]

For example the Father is love, the Son manifests love, and the
Spirit makes that love effective. The Father initiated the word, the Son
becomes the word, and the Spirit causes the hearing and the seeing of
the word. The Holy Spirit is the power and the efficacy of everything
we need to live a godly life, initiated by the Father, and accessed more
and more as we know Jesus better.

So what keeps us from knowing Jesus better? What keeps us from
accessing his divine power that gives us everything we need to live a
godly life? I believe it's because as we approach Jesus we come with
our list of conditions, things we are not willing to give up, things
we are not willing to have crucified in our life. We have come to
falsely believe that God wants us to have a comfortable life more than
a crucified life. Whenever we exhibit a disposition that is contrary to
Jesus, especially towards others, we cause the Holy Spirit to grieve
(Ephesians 4:30) and his power is inaccessible.

Imagine you are dying of some terrible disease. So you go to the
doctor and the doctor says, I have a remedy for you. If you just follow
my advice you will be healed and you will live a long and fruitful life,
but there's only one problem: while you're taking my remedy you
can't eat chocolate. But then you say, forget it! No chocolate? What's
the use of living? I'll follow the doctor's remedy, but I will also keep
eating chocolate.

You see if Christ is really God, then the list of our conditions are
gone. To know Jesus Christ is to say, "anywhere God's will touches

my life, anywhere Jesus' word speaks", I will say, "Lord I will obey."
There are no conditions anymore. If he's really God, He can't just be
a supplement to help us get what we want and we can't assume we've
entered into a no obligation relationship. To know Jesus is to come to
him and say, "Lord I'm willing to let you start a complete reordering
of my life."

The church may be culpable in this as well, when it unintentionally
preaches self-denial while practicing a consumeristic form of church,
catering to an ideology that sees personal freedom and comfort as the
highest human good. We must be cautious of trivializing the gospel,
of presenting it in a form that compromises its radical message. If
someone is accustom to seeing or hearing about a product that promises to improve their life, they may begin to think that Christ will improve their life in the same commercial way. Christ can become just
another consumer item vying for our attention. He no longer speaks
as crucified King, but as a slick salesman; not as Lord of the universe,
but as a marketing genius. Such consumerism trivializes the message
and suffocates our understanding of the gospel. The truth of God is
rich and full of grace. We cannot box up and market the great truths
of our Lord. [33]

In this pluralistic culture we live in, we are exposed to a plethora
of worldviews, which all claim to have a version of the truth that will
help us make sense of this world - a world that calls us to seek gratification, pleasure, and entertainment, all that we may live a comfortable life. Seeing our Christian faith as a product to consume is a false
teaching that has inadvertently crept into the church from our challenging culture. The late John Stott believed that "choosing the easy
trail, the road most taken, and the path of least resistance can only end
in mediocrity, even if it comes from praise." [34]

We can be tempted to surrender to the culture's teaching of tolerance that believes the standards of God are an outdated burden and
an unnecessary judgment that limits our freedom. Coupled with the
pressure to live as God desires, without wanting to stand out from the

crowd, it is easier to travel the road of comfort and popularity. It's in the midst of this temptation and pressure that we need to draw on the power of Christ.

This is the challenging culture that God is using as His way of melting the impurities in our lives that seek this life of comfort. It is the antithesis of God's design for the church to live as a citizen of his kingdom. God's purpose for the Body of Christ is to be a faithful expression of His Kingdom, rooted in God's gospel of grace, and growing the church in the knowledge of Jesus Christ, to participate in God's mission. It is there and only there we find His divine power that gives us everything we need for living a holy and godly life.

"Faith in God is not just believing he exists, but
doing what he says because you believe he will keep
his promises."
B. Clayton Bell, Christian Reader, Vol. 32, no. 2.

CHAPTER 2 - THE WORLD'S INSECURITY OR GOD'S PROMISES

Years ago Wende and I set up 529 college funds for all our grandchildren. It won't come close to paying for all of their college education but it will help. It is money we put in trust for them until they go to college. Our oldest, Kyra, received her portion and finished college this past year, graduating from Eastern University. The rest of the grandchildren are either in college or will be using the money soon. It is not in a legal sense an irrevocable trust, that is, we can technically change it. However, it is irrevocable in our minds, because we made a promise to give the money for a specific use to a specific person. So even when I take the Smith grandchildren to a Pittsburgh Steelers game against Indianapolis and they root for the Colts, because it was their father's favorite team, we can't change this irrevocable trust. Even if our grandsons choose a college we don't like, we can't change this trust, we can't change the promise. The only standard that is binding is the promise of the money being used for their college education. The promise doesn't change based on how well they deal with the circumstances of life or the choices they make in God's holy kingdom.

Living as a citizen of the kingdom in our challenging culture becomes like a crucible that melts ores and metals to separate out impurities. The impurities in Peter's second letter is the church's complacency, their self satisfaction, and the false teachings that were twisting the truth. Again it is unclear whether the false teaching enabled a self-satisfied refusal to grow in God's grace or whether the churches complacency opened the door for the twisting of the truth. Either way Peter has started his letter with revisiting some foundational truths about the gospel. He jumps right in to tell us that in the power of Christ we have everything we need to live a godly life. At the moment of salvation, God gave us a royal gift in the person of the Holy Spirit who is the power and the efficacy of everything we need to live a life pleasing to God. And God's grace didn't stop there. Along with a divine power to live a godly life comes the rich and wonderful promises of God. So Peter writes in verse 1:4, "And by that same mighty power he has given us all of his rich and wonderful promises. He has promised that you will escape the decadence all around you caused by evil desires and that you will share in his divine nature."

This is the second great resource God makes available to us in his grace - the power of Christ, now the promises of Christ. The theme of promises runs throughout the entire Bible, starting with the promise God made in the garden of Eden, that Adam and Eve's disastrous sin and fall would not determine our destiny. The fall in the garden would not be the end of humanity's story. And throughout the rest of salvation history, God unfolds His promises to His people. Peter summarizes those promises into two general categories in this verse. [35]

First is the promise of escape: "He has promised that you will escape the decadence all around you, caused by evil desires." The promise is not an escape from the physical world or from the trials and tribulations of this world. It is an escape from sin. Living in this world, even in this challenging culture, is a good thing. There are many enjoyable blessings to be found and experienced, but we are not to so identify with the world we live in, that we stop fleeing from the sin in it. The sin which is in rebellion to God's redemptive purposes and which can destroy us. We don't pretend to be perfect, which would make the promises of escape unnecessary, and we don't say we don't need to be perfect which would make the promise cheap.

What we can say is that we will be perfect and that makes the promises of Christ rich and wonderful. Paul writes in 1 Corinthians 10:13, "The temptations in your life are no different from what others experience. And God is faithful. He will not allow the temptation to be more than you can stand. When you are tempted, he will show you a way out so that you can endure."

The word temptation can either mean an enticement to evil or it can mean testing in general, including all kinds of trials and tribulations. God does not entice us to do evil but does test us. Satan entices and always with evil intent. So God can and will test us by allowing Satan to entice us towards evil. But God's promise here is that He will not allow the temptation or the test to go beyond our ability to resist and overcome. In other words, God puts a limit on the temptation or the test by always providing a way of escape. A way of escape is the picture of an army trapped in the mountains, but escapes a seemingly impossible situation through a pass. This temptation or test is that place God uses to separate out the impurities in our life. God's irrevocable promise is to bring us into a deeper relationship with himself through this trial.

The second promise Peter mentions is the promise of glory. He writes, "that you will share in his divine nature." Now let's be clear, Peter is not suggesting we will become little gods. We must always preserve the distance between our Creator God and those he creates. Yet the very purpose of the gospel and this promise is that we are to grow more and more into the likeness of Christ, restoring the image of God created in us, but broken in the fall. We will either share the image or character of those being judged or the image or character of the one who does the judging. God has promised we will share in his image or character. Paul wrote in Romans chapter eight that we have been adopted as sons and daughters so that we might be conformed to the likeness of God's own son (Romans 8:29).

This is God's undeserved generosity, the promise of escape and the promise of glory. The promises of Christ and the power of Christ, everything we need to live a life pleasing to God. Now here is where we all nod and say "amen." However, shortly we will go out into the world. You will put this book down or we will leave church on Sunday morning and we can become like Peter, who Jesus bids to walk on the water, to leave the security of the boat, and where the storms begin to overwhelm our understanding of Christ's power and Christ's promises. Quickly Christ and the gospel feel insufficient for our everyday experiences in this challenging culture and before we know it we are listening to a different gospel, a philosophy or ideology, that offers to make sense of our world. A desire for comfort overtakes our good intentions for living a Kingdom life.

A number of years ago an author and researcher named Maxwell Malta wrote something called *Psycho Cybernetics*. [36] His book became the foundation for many self-help books and motivational speakers. In it he estimates that 95% of people in our society today are insecure. My assumption is that the other 5% are just not telling the truth. All you have to do is look at the world around us. We really have little or no control over much of our lives, mostly because we live in a sinful and broken world. If we are alive, we all have some degree of insecurity and Malta documented the causes of that insecurity into three general experiences. These are experiences that I would conclude are simply the result of our sinful nature and the world we live in, yet the categories can be helpful.

The first is the experience of childhood. Having not received enough encouragement and affirmation, it left many adults trying to achieve perfection or at least trying to avoid failures. The second is the experience of change. We live in a mobile society. We move if we don't like the weather, we run from difficult situations, and we change churches, jobs and spouses at the drop of a hat. Lastly is the experience of crisis. The death of a loved one, being the victim of a crime, along with divorce, illness, and financial struggles, are all experiences that can contribute to our insecurity.

If we can't readily identify with the causes of our insecurity - experiences of childhood, change and crisis - then the author suggests we may be able to identify with the symptoms: aggressive, addictive or affective behavior. Aggressive is the type A personality; competitive, work dominated, and impatient. All of this is coming from our insecurities. Addictive behavior is dependent upon someone or something, a behavior that needs to maintain the high because we can't face the low. Affective behavior compensates for our insecurities by criticizing others or withdrawing from them. The point is, much of our behavior is rooted in insecurity and it hinders us from living a godly life. Instead of seeking the latest pop psychology, let's look at a couple of examples in Scripture of some insecure situations overcome by the security of God's promises.

In Acts 27 the storm had probably gone on for two weeks. They were hungry from lack of food, the ship was breaking up, and they hadn't seen the sun or stars for days. That's some real insecurity. But then Paul brings some good news. God has promised, not one person is going to die. You're going to be shipwrecked on an island. You're going to enter into God's crucible, but no one dies! God promised and Paul believed it. It is basically the message of the Gospel. God promises and we believe. It's the same for our circumstances, whether it's the experience of childhood, change, or crisis. In the midst of insecurity we lay hold of God's promises. The promises may not change the insecure circumstances, but the secure promises of God changes our insecurities.

The second story, from Genesis 12, is about a man in a well developed city called Ur, who is called by God to leave everything that is familiar and go to an unknown land. Now if I was Abram, I would be thinking, can you be a little more specific? Why should I do this? What's it going to be like there? Am I going to be sleeping in a Holiday Inn or camping in a tent? But Abram went because he believed in God's promises, and God continued to give Abram promises that he was asked to trust. The most daunting promise was that at 100 years old and married to a barren wife, they would have a child. Abram laughed, but God said trust me, my promise is good, so he believed and Isaac was born. Yet years later Abraham is asked by God to test that promise by offering up his only son as a sacrifice. Now God had promised that Abraham would be the father of many nations, but how would that promise be fulfilled if he kills Isaac? Well Abraham was so confident in God's promise, he reasoned that if he was obedient to God in offering Isaac as a sacrifice, God would raise his son from the dead. As we know at the last second God provides a lamb from the thicket to be the sacrifice instead of Isaac.

God is the only source of our true security because of His promises - not promises of a red or blue ideology, nor the philosophy of a self help guru and not even the appeal of a prosperity gospel or a well tuned worship experience. So many lives and relationships self-destruct because as insecure people we don't deal with our insecurity or we seek one of the many false promises the world offers. The only way to deal with our insecurity is to find security in the promises of Christ. It is impossible for God to lie, it is impossible for God to go back on his promises or not to fulfill his promises. Listen to what Paul says about this in Galatians 3:15-18,

> Dear brothers and sisters, here's an example from every day life. Just as no one can set aside or amend an irrevocable agreement so it is in this case. God gave the promise to Abraham and his child. And noticed that it doesn't say the promise was to his children, as if it met many descendants but the promise was to his child, and that of course means Christ. This is what I am trying to say: the agreement God made with Abraham could not be canceled 430 years later when God gave the law to Moses. God would be breaking his promise. For if the inheritance could be received only by keeping the law, then it would not be the

result of excepting God's promise. But God gave it to Abraham as a promise.

Just as our grandkids can't do anything wrong to change our irrevocable promise of their college funds, Paul is saying because God gave his promise to Abraham 430 years before the law even existed, then how well we keep the law has no bearing on the promises. God's irrevocable trust, much more dependable then our promise to our grandkids, was established before the standards of a godly life were given. Paul wants us to see the unconditional nature of the promises made to Abraham and show us that we are the beneficiaries of those promises. And all of these promises find their fulfillment in Christ (Galatians 3:29).

Maybe you have heard people refer to Christianity as a crutch for wimps. Well you know what? They are right! Christianity is a crutch because we were all wimps without Christ. We were drifting without an anchor. We are all insecure, we can't save ourselves, we can't keep ourselves alive, we can't fit ourselves for heaven, we can't reconcile ourselves to God, we can't undo what we've done and we can't do what we should be doing. We are a bunch of insecure wimps. And until we understand fully God's unchanging promises and come to him in all our weakness, we remain drifters in need of an anchor and cripples in need of a crutch. The power of Christ has given us the promises of Christ and the writer of Hebrews says, "This confidence is like a strong and trustworthy anchor for our souls. It leads us through the curtain of heaven into God's inner sanctuary" (Hebrews 6:19).

"Maturity is pressing towards the mark; immaturity is
complacency and self-satisfaction."
Roberta Hestenes, Leadership , vol. 9, no 4.

CHAPTER 3 - A CHEAP GRACE OR CHRISTIAN GROWTH

In nearly 40 years of life and ministry in the inner city, I found my self teaching how so many well meaning Christians would unknowingly apply the term ROI, "return on investment," to their efforts in our ministry. If they were going to invest in a person or a program they expected a proper return on their time or energy spent. An improvement on a report card, the appropriate thankful attitude, or a change in some addictive behavior; some measurement of success was expected for their gracious efforts. The law of achievement was being applied to a people ruled by poverty and violence, whose skin was often considered the wrong color to succeed and who had little hope that any of this would change. It contradicted the very nature of the gospel. It asked people to justify the help they received with some measure of achievement and if they failed it continued to shatter their dignity and envelop them in despair. However, the gospel taught them that they were not defined by these outside influences of the law, a gospel we attempted to not only proclaim but to embody in our church and community.

Let's be honest, sometimes we have difficulty understanding the correlation between grace and the law, understanding what Christian freedom is. We struggle to find the balance between the extremes of legalism, attempting to earn God's favor, and the extremes of libertinism, abusing God's favor, a cheap grace. There are those who teach that someone is justified before God by their works and on the other side those who believe that if you are saved, your behavior does not matter. Rarely, of course, are these extremes what we actually see to-day, but rather some continuum that leans in one direction or the other - a leaning that can shift in order to make our version of the gospel fit more comfortably into our circumstances. It is like the young boy who wrote on the board, $5 + 3 = 10$, and then says "it may not be right but it works for me." We often apply the legal approach to judge others and the gracious approach to excuse our particular sinful behaviors.

Consequently we end up with a belief and behavior, a confession and conduct, a profession and practice, that don't always line up. There's a gap between our talk and our walk. There's a disconnect between our Sunday faith and our Monday work. We apply legal expectations on others while giving ourselves grace without repentance. Peter's goal in this letter is to bridge that gap by teaching us that God has given us the capacity to do what he asks. In fact, God will not even ask us to do any thing until he gives us all that is necessary. God's grace, in Christ's power and promises, has given us everything we need, so now Peter says "Make every effort to apply the benefits of these promises to your life..." (2 Peter 1:5a). In other words, walk the talk, practice our profession, behave according to our beliefs, conduct ourselves like citizens of God's holy kingdom. Live a godly life on Sunday and every day.

Peter wanted to challenge the complacent and comfortable Christians, who in listening to the false teachers of their day, had begun to believe that because salvation was not from good works, they could live as they pleased. However, the growth for Christians comes from rolling up the sleeves of grace and putting it to work. Having been given all that is needed, there is now nothing more important than to give ourselves to developing our Christian life. Every morning the moment our feet hit the floor, God sends us out to our respective mission fields of family care, neighbor loving, and holy vocations, to put his grace to work. God has done his part and now it is time for us to do ours.

That grace works when we make it a priority to exercise our Christian faith. God's gift of Christ's power and promises are in contrast with merit but not with effort. The practice of Christian grace is to exert ourselves. The grace of Christians does more than belong, it participates, it does more than care, it helps, it does more than forgive, it reconciles, it does more than dream, it creates, it does more than teach, it inspires, it does more than give, it serves, it does more than suffer, it triumphs, it does more than live, it grows.

"So make every effort," Peter says in verse five. If your faith is real, it will work itself out in public and practical ways because our faith is both foundational and functional. God has worked in everything we need, now we are called to work it out. Peter uses a Greek word here translated "effort" that means to do it in haste and in zeal. In other words, Peter is saying do it now, make it a priority, to apply the benefits of the power and promises of Christ in every aspect of our lives. Apply it to our job, our neighbors, and our families. Worship God with the same zeal on Monday as we do on Sunday.

Our widowed daughter, at the time, had been asked by some neighborhood teens to borrow her family's portable basketball hoop for a community outreach, put on by our church. She agreed and the boys emptied the water from the base and carried it the two blocks to the church. At the end of the day she asked them to again empty the water from the base, return it to her driveway and fill the base with water. They did all that, but neglected to put the water back in the base. When our daughter returned home she found the basketball hoop lying through the front windshield, with a dented hood, on her brand new van. She now had a choice to make in how she would respond. She had a right go to their parents and ask for some financial payment to cover the insurance deductible, but which may have also resulted in some unnecessary punishment at home, or she could forgive and maintain the relationship she had developed with these urban teens. She chose the later. Our daughter made it a priority, made every effort, to be in a relationship over being right and the only way we can do that kind of thing is because God has given us everything we need to roll up our sleeves and make grace work.

Peter says, "apply the benefits." I want you to see something important in this passage before we go any further. The Greek word Peter uses in "apply the benefits" in verse five is the same word he uses in verse 11 where he says "and God will" or literally you will be provided with. So let's understand this. In verse five "apply the benefits" and verse 11 "God will provide;" we exert the grace out by applying the benefits and then God provides the grace back in. "Will provide" is in the passive voice, it is being done by God to us. It is a Greek word that acts like bookends to this passage and conveys the meaning of an extremely generous giver.[37] You see, in the practice of Christians we are cooperating with the grace of God. That's how grace works, without thinking about the cost of our exertion, because it's all God's grace. It didn't cost us anything to get it and it doesn't cost us anything to give it.

That's how a single mom can say I want to have a relationship with some neighborhood teens more than she wants to be right or be reimbursed. It doesn't cost anything to do that because God already provided what it cost to do such a gracious thing. That's how we can go two miles when we were asked to go only one. That's how we can give our coat when only our shirt was requested. We can exert ourselves to do the extra, we can make it a priority, because we have already been given everything we need.

As part of this effort Peter lists a number of virtues we are to add to our Christian walk. He describes them as a series of steps in our spiritual growth, not necessarily in a precise order, but nonetheless each one is as important as the others. It may be significant, however, that he began with faith and ended with love. Faith as the foundational virtue of Christianity that, as the Apostle James reminds us, always goes further to develop additional characteristics that are then all bound together in love. From our base of faith we add our knowledge of God, self control over the lust for sin, endurance to remain steadfast in the challenge of today's culture, godliness to honor Christ in every aspect of life, and lovingkindness for our friends and neighbors. We are to have these qualities in "increasing measures." In other words, it is not enough to be content with just being a Christian who has their ticket punched to heaven. A true Christian is never comfortable resting with a minimal effort but is always working towards the goal of reflecting a life of Christlikeness.

Peter taught us that to enable the work of grace, we must first make it our priority and second he tells us to measure our progress. One of the ways grace rolls up its sleeves and works, is an increasing dissatisfaction with the level of our growth in godliness. The verb grow in verse eight is from a noun meaning estate or property. It means we possess property or have access to an estate that is fully at our disposal. [38]

We have a responsibility to grow that estate and to do so in such a way that it is useful to others; useful to your church, your vocation, your neighbor and your family. Peter is convinced that true knowledge of Christ is not irrelevant book knowledge but rather a knowledge of Christ that produces change in us and others, as well as in the systems and organizations we are called to participate. In other words, we should be able to measure our progress. We should be able to see visible evidence of change and growth in our lives and in the lives of those around us, including a dissatisfaction with the status quo. Too many Christians are content with simply being a Christian, happy we're not going to hell and satisfied with being a Christian consumer. The true knowledge Peter is writing about creates a thirst to know Christ better and to use that knowledge to become productive and useful as a citizen of God's advancing kingdom.

When he was 48 years old, Johan Sebastian Bach acquired a copy of Martin Luther's three volume translation of the Bible. He poured over it as if it was a long lost treasure. He underlined passages and made notes in the margins, even correcting some errors and inserting some missing words. One author wrote that Bach the musician was a

Christian who lived with the Bible. The Baroque era's greatest organist and composer, and one of the most productive geniuses in the history of western music, was really first and foremost a theologian who was called to work with the keyboard. One of Bach's favorite Bible verses read, "The trumpeters and singers performed together in unison to praise and give thanks to the Lord. Accompanied by trumpets, cymbals, and other instruments, they raised their voices and praised the Lord with these words: 'He is good. His faithful love endures forever'! At that moment a thick cloud filled the Temple of the Lord" (2 Chronicles 5:13).

Bach wrote this in the margin of his Bible, "At a reverent performance of music, God is always at hand with his gracious presence." [39] We could substitute a "reverent performance of music" with "every reverent endeavor of our lives" God is at hand with his gracious presence. Peter's point is that the practice of Christians means being an effective Christian in every endeavor of our lives, not settling for mediocrity or not being complacent and taking the path of least resistance. That's where dreams die and hope fades and Peter says that's where we become blind or at least shortsighted. The word blind here is a willful blindness, we close our eyes intentionally, forgetting what God has done for us. It's not just a mental process of forgetting, it's a practical failure to take into account the significance of something. In other words we haven't forgotten, we have failed to act. Peter is warning about the dangers of complacency, of standing still in the Christian life. If we are not moving forward, we are falling behind and we become disabled, blind, and shortsighted. We are blind to our present spiritual state, we are squinting to see the future and we have forgotten God's grace in the past. So Peter says measure your progress, see if you are actually becoming productive and useful in the mission of God's Kingdom.

Make it a priority, measure our progress, and lastly maintain our perspective. He writes, "So, dear brothers and sisters, work hard to prove that you really are among those God has called and chosen. Do these things, and you will never fall away. Then God will give you a grand entrance into the eternal Kingdom of our Lord and Savior Jesus Christ" (2 Peter 1:10-11).

Peter reinforces his "make every effort" with "work hard." Work hard to prove your calling as a citizen of the kingdom and being chosen by God before the creation of the world. The word prove has a legal connotation. It means to ratify something. Called and chosen are not some abstract or irrelevant theological terms, they are the context of our hope and the expression of God's sovereignty and thus require evidence of their existence. So Peter says work hard to prove it. If we do God gives us two eternal promises. First we will never stumble or fall away, not that we will never sin. It literally means we will never suffer a reverse because God will never change his mind, nor send us back because we are not good enough. We will never fall out of grace, we will only fall into God's grace. Our citizenship in the kingdom is secure. The second eternal promise is that God will open wide the gates of heaven. It's the picture of a victorious marathon runner being welcomed to the finish line by a cheering home crowd. It's not God repaying a price to us because we have worked hard but rather God providing an eternal home for those who have maintained their perspective.

Sam Shoemaker, in a speech on the anniversary of the founding of alcoholics anonymous said,

> You know what a lot of religious people are like? They are like a lot of people sitting around a railroad station thinking they are on a train. Everybody is talking about travel, and you hear the names of the stations, and you have got the tickets, and there is the smell of baggage around you and a great deal of stir, and if you sit there long enough you almost think you are on a train. But you are not. You only start to get converted at that point where you get on the train and

get pulled out of the station. And you do get pulled out; you do not walk out in your own power. [40]

Peter says we have every thing we need. We have our ticket, the train is in the station, our bags are packed, all we have to do is get on board. Growing Christians, citizens of God's kingdom, roll up their sleeves and put God's grace to work. They get on board with God's mission in this world, and in His church, with our vocations, our families and with our neighbors. He has provided all we need, but the question remains are we on board?

"The lack of scriptural knowledge is the source of all evils in the church."
John Chrysostom. *Leadership*, Vol. 16, no. 2.

CHAPTER 4 - GOD'S MANUAL FOR GROWING CHRISTIANS

There is a relatively new religion invented by a Massachusetts psychologist that has been gaining some popularity over recent years. Called Yoism, this system of beliefs is based on the open source principle, where the general public becomes a combined, creative authority and source of truth. One example of the open source phenomenon is the successful online encyclopedia known as Wikipedia. Yoism operates and evolves over the Internet, and has numerous contributors. It shuns traditional religious authorities and eschews divine inspiration in favor of the wisdom of man. Albert Einstein and Sigmund Freud are among its most revered saints. Dan Kriegman, who founded Yoism, did so because he wanted to make religion open to change and responsive to the wisdom of all people. "I don't think anyone has ever complained about something that didn't lead to some revision or clarification in the book of Yoism", said Kriegman. He added, "Every aware and conscious spirit is divine and has direct access to the truth... Open source embodies that. There is no authority." [41]

Although not well known, this is an example of Peter's concern. That this kind of teaching is not just in our challenging culture today, but philosophically has crept into some churches, chipping away at the authority of God's word. When we become self-satisfied, we become susceptible to truth-twisting and when we become lazy in our faith it's often because we have avoided truth. The twisting of truth or the avoidance of truth, either or both, can contribute to a downward spiral of Christian complacency to spiritual stagnation. That is why

Peter reminds his readers, in 2 Peter 1:12-21, that his teaching did not come from some clever made up stories but rather from God himself. The ultimate authority over our lives is not us, but rather the revelation of God in Scripture.

The pony express was created in 1860 to move mail across the United States from Saint Joseph, Missouri to Sacramento, California. The express was designed to be completed in 10 mile legs, because it was understood that that was as far as a horse could gallop. So a rider would ride his horse for 10 miles and at the next stop would dismount and get on another horse, ride another 10 miles, dismount, and so on. A rider would complete 7 to 10 of those legs before a different rider would take over the work. In that fashion the mail could get across country, 2000 miles, in about 10 to 14 days. This was the mail delivery system. And in order to conserve weight and make the Pony Express system efficient, the riders had to be less than 125 pounds. Saddles had to be very small, kind of economical saddles. The horses' hooves were shod with very lightweight shoes or no shoes at all. The mail that was sent had to be very, very thin and people were charged exorbitant mailing rates. Riders were allowed to carry only a few small provisions with them. Yet for all of the concern that the Pony Express had for weight conservation, every single one of the riders were sent out with a full sized Bible. The Pony Express valued and viewed the word of God as absolutely essential for the journey on the trail. [42]

Peter clearly wants to emphasize the importance of Scripture. He plans to keep on reminding his readers and working hard to make things clear about what he saw and heard, about the authenticity and reliability of the truth. Peter starts by establishing two eyewitness testimonies, the apostles in the New Testament and the prophets in the Old Testament. He points to the transfiguration experience he had with James and John, where he saw Jesus' majestic splendor and heard God's voice say, "This is my beloved Son and I am fully pleased with him, listen to him" (Mathew 17:5b). Peter saw Jesus' transfigured body and heard God's voice, an historical event and an experiential account that defends the authority and authenticity of Scripture.

Then Peter says, because of that, we have even greater confidence in the message proclaimed by the prophets. So pay close attention to what they wrote, for their words are like a light shining in the darkness. Peter had heard and seen a partial fulfillment of what the Old Testament prophets wrote about the coming of Jesus as the Messiah. The Old Testament was pregnant with the gospel of Jesus Christ and Peter was witnessing its birth.

Jackson was not supposed to be our youngest grandchild but his twin cousins were forced to come into this world earlier than expected. Our daughter-in-law Katrina had preeclampsia, a life threatening condition that required giving birth to her twin boys nearly two months early. It was touch and go for all three, mother and the boys. There were a few terrifying hours before we knew Katrina was going to survive and then a few days before Alex was safe, but a few weeks before we knew Zach was out of the woods. Our son and family had hope and was comforted by prayers and expressions of love, but that hope and comfort had no effect on the actual state of affairs. We had no guarantee from God or anyone that our daughter-in-law and grandsons would be all right. That assurance only came when we were told by the doctors that they were actually alive and were going to be fine. You see faith does not make something true, faith only embraces what is true. We have faith in the gospel of Jesus Christ because His life and His ministry, His death and resurrection, are completed events in history and not some clever made up story. That is what Peter is teaching us. The Old Testament was full of hope and comfort in the prophet's message about the coming Messiah. But that hope and comfort didn't find its fulfillment until Christ showed up. Until Christ, the Old Testament was just a shadow of what was to come, but now that we have written eyewitness accounts of the actual person and work of Christ, the Old Testament takes on even more significance. So Peter says pay close attention to it.

What Peter has done in this text is tie the Old Testament and the New Testament into one complete story about God, the unfolding revelation of the God of creation and his redemptive work in history. And here is the most important thing: the story is autobiographical. The story is not only about God, it is from God. The Bible we hold in our hands is God's intellectual property. In other words the Bible did not have its origin in the will, the impulse, or the initiative of any human being. The Bible came from God. The prophets, or even King David, did not all of a sudden decide maybe I should start writing down some things that would be helpful to my family or my neighbors. No! Peter says no prophecy in Scripture ever came from the prophet's own ideas or interpretations, it came from God. The theological term for this is inspiration. "All Scripture is inspired by God and is useful to teach us what is true and to make us realize what is wrong in our lives. It corrects us when we are wrong and teaches us to do what is right" (2 Timothy 3:16).

This reinforces exactly what Peter is saying - all Scripture is inspired by God. Literally all Scripture is God-breathed. It was brought into existence by God's breath, by God's Holy Spirit. The Bible's origin is from God's mind, reflecting God's life and language. It is why it is rightly called God's word.

When God created the world, he spoke things into existence - water, light and the mountains. But when God created man he took the soil of the earth and he breathed. He breathed life into us so that we would reflect His image and set us apart from the rest of His creation. Consequently, when we understand that it was the same breath of God that gave us the Bible, we don't just have a great book, we have the holy word of the living God. God's very nature has been breathed into the Scriptures.

Now there are two important conclusions we can make from the inspiration of Scripture. The first is that the Bible is truthful. If it comes from God it reflects the character of God. God cannot lie, God is righteous and just, God is without error. Thus, if the Bible comes from God, then it too is without error. If the Bible is inspired, if it is God-breathed, it is also inerrant, it is without error and also infallible, it is unable to commit an error. We cannot say the Bible is from God and then claim it has errors in it. Now are there transcribed errors in the years of translations from the original text? Yes, but just like I can write a truthful letter with misspelled words and poor grammar, transcribed errors do not adversely affect the truth of the Bible.

The second conclusion we can come to from our God-breathed Bible is that it is useful. If the Bible is from God and is truthful, you soon discover it is also useful. If I have information that tells me a show starts at 7 PM but when I arrive I discovered it actually started at 5 PM or if my itinerary tells me my plane leaves at 3 PM but in fact it was 1 PM and I missed my flight, that untruthful information was not very useful. But because the Bible is truthful in everything, I can count on it to be useful to me in every aspect of life, to guide me, to motivate me, to challenge me, to transform me and to equip me for every good work.

The prime meridian is the earth's zero degrees longitude dividing it into the eastern and western hemispheres. The prime meridian came about through the work of John Flamsteed, the first astronomer royal, who made it his life mission to produce a proper navigational chart of the heavens, mapping the locations of thousands of stars. Eventually based on Flamsteed's work, scientists were able to help people find their position on the planet, allowing them to answer that fundamental question of philosophy and physics; where am I? The power of the prime meridian is that it is a fixed position through which our knowledge of time and place can be understood. This is a metaphor for the effect of the Bible in human life. The Scripture is our meridian. It is the fixed position, given by God himself, through which we can understand who we are, where we are, and where we must go from here.

So the Bible is God-breathed, its author is God, and therefore it is truthful and useful. That addresses the who, but what about the how? How did God author the Bible? We have been told Moses wrote the first five books of the Bible, most of the Psalms were written by David, Paul wrote the biggest chunk of the New Testament and we're reading from the letter written by Peter. Well, inspiration doesn't mean dictation. Peter said it was the Holy Spirit who moved the prophets to speak, they were carried along by the Holy Spirit. It means the Holy Spirit superintended the writers of Scripture, the Holy Spirit protected the writers so that the end result was exactly what God wanted them to write. Read what Luke says about writing his gospel account, in 1:1-4:

> Many people have set out to write accounts about the events that have been fulfilled among us. They used the eyewitness reports circulating among us from the early disciples. Having carefully investigated everything from the beginning, I also have decided to write an accurate account for you, most honorable Theophilus, so you can be certain of the truth of everything you were taught.

So God didn't say to Luke sit down and write what I tell you word for word. God superintended Luke to write down the truth God wanted to convey, while protecting Luke's individual style and personality. Martin Lloyd Jones writes, "These men were so controlled by the Holy Spirit that they were safeguarded from error; they were guided not only to a knowledge of the truth, but in their expression of the truth. Their own personality was given free play, but it was controlled by the Holy Spirit, and that guaranteed this ultimate result." [43]

We started a community development corporation connected to the urban church we had planted, which enabled us to build and rehab affordable housing in the neighborhood. We did what is called a design build. We were the developer and an architect was the general contractor who hired and supervised many different sub contractors. Sometimes based on schedules and availability we even had different plumbers. One plumber would install the sink first and then the toilet while a different plumber might do just the reverse but the finished product and job were done just as the architect had designed it. In the same way God was the design builder of Scripture, He directed and moved in the lives of the Old and New Testament writers, to reflect exactly, without error, what He had designed.

Yet there are some, even Christians, who are inclined to agree with the atheist scientist Lawrence Krauss, who quipped, "The Bible was written basically before people knew anything." [44] In other words the Bible may have been truthful for the ancient near East, but it's not relative for our enlightened culture. So we end up picking and choosing what we think is appropriate for us and the culture we live in. Yet have we ever considered how appropriate or inappropriate a particular scripture is for other cultures? Tim Keller, in one of his sermons, explains how the Bible contradicts and challenges every culture at some point:

> In individualistic, Western societies, we read the Bible, and we have a problem with what it says about sex. But then we read what the Bible says about forgiveness—'forgive your enemy;''forgive your brother seventy times seven;" "turn the other cheek;' 'when your enemy asks for your shirt, give him your cloak as well'—and we say, 'How wonderful!' It's because we are driven by a culture of guilt. But if you were to go to the Middle East, they would think that what the Bible has to say about sex is pretty good. (Actually, they might feel it's not strict enough!) But when they would read what the Bible says about forgiving your enemies, it would strike them as absolutely crazy. It's because their culture is not an individualistic society like ours. It's more of a shame culture than a guilt culture. Let me ask you a question: If you're offended

by something in the Bible, why should your cultural
sensibilities trump everybody else's? Why should we
get rid of the Bible because it offends your culture? [45]

What Keller is pointing out is that the Bible is not the product of
any one culture and as a result it will offend some aspect of every culture. We can not pick and choose what we want to believe and reject
the rest because we think it is offensive or irrelevant to our present
culture. If we believe God is the author of the Bible and therefore
is inspired, inerrant and infallible, it is reasonable to believe it will
challenge and even offend our cultural sensibilities. To reject that authority leaves us with a god of our own making. Diogenes Allen tells
us, "The Latin root of 'authority' and 'authentic' means 'that which
allows growth and life.' Our resentment of the authority of God in
Christ is, therefore, foolish." [46]

God's authority in Scripture does not contradict a personal relationship with Him but rather is a precondition for it. It is a precondition for our relationship with God and the foundation for growing
Christians in the God designed trial of our challenging culture. Again
as Jones writes, "I either accept this Book and its verities, or I base my
life and view of the future upon the thoughts and ideas and insights
and understandings of men. And as I am confronted by these alternatives, I say for myself that I am driven to believe this Word." [47]

The good news is that Peter has told us we have everything we need
to live out a growing relationship with a living God. God has provided
the power and promises of Christ and instructed us to make every
effort to apply those benefits in order to prove we have them. Those
efforts begin and end with God's manual for growing Christians, an
instruction manual on how to live a kingdom holiness.

PART 2 - WARNINGS FOR THE CHURCH

"I believe a very large majority of churchgoers are merely unthinking, slumbering worshipers of an unknown God." Charles H. Spurgeon in Metropolitan Tabernacle Pulpit, Vol. 11. Christianity Today, Vol. 40, no. 1.

CHAPTER 5 - CAUTIONS FOR THE COMFORTABLE CHURCH

A number of years ago I read an article in the Pittsburgh Tribune Review, by Salena Zito, who was reflecting on the controversy surrounding the New England Patriots and their quarterback Tom Brady, concerning the deflating of footballs for the Super Bowl. She was asking if this is the picture of where we are as a society? She wrote, "Are we all just trying to game the system, whatever system we are in, just to get ahead? On the surface we look like a country with a tired soul, tolerant of cheating, poor sportsmanship, and mediocrity. Where are the leaders who take on corruption, who find ways to rebuild communities, and pass on the tradition of faith in our society?" [48]

Zito is describing the complacency Peter has been inferring in his second letter. Settling for good enough instead of striving for well done. The gospel of Christ is not just for making us a good moral person or to make us happy and healthy. The Gospel has been given to birth and grow churches, the body of Christ, a community of believers, to be change agents for God's kingdom and to be a part of God's redeeming work to bring shalom to the world we live in.

Up to this point Peter has offered great encouragement and instruction on how to avail ourselves to all we need to please God by our holy living. But if his first chapter was the carrot, then chapter two is the whip, cautioning us against getting carried away by the error of false teachings. And it is our complacency and comfort that so often makes us gullible to those who cleverly teach their destructive heresies about God.

So in this second chapter, Peter starts by writing in verse one, "But there were also false prophets in Israel." Peter has previously explained that we have true teachers in the New Testament apostles and the Old Testament prophets, giving us the complete story about God and from God. He contrasts this to verse three and the made up "clever lies" of these false teachers. Peter tells us there was and there will be false teachers among us. Commenting on this passage John Calvin wrote, "The Spirit of God has declared once and for all that the church will never be free from this internal trouble". [49]

The presentation of untruths and half-truths is and will forever be a present and inevitable danger in any church or denomination. Fewer than one in four Americans (24%) now believe the Bible is "the actual word of God, and is similar to the 26% who view it as a book of fables, legends, history and moral precepts recorded by man." [50] In other words, fewer people believe the Bible is written by God and without error. That becomes a real seedbed for misleading people about God and following such untruths has some serious consequences.

So how do we recognize false teaching? How do we avoid the influence of this misdirected instruction? Such teachers don't usually wear a sign around their neck declaring "I am of false teacher, don't listen to me." It's usually just the opposite. They are often presenting plausible and popular ideas, while quietly introducing or smuggling in their falsehoods. What is taught is more than a permissible variant of the gospel. Peter emphasizes this by adding the word destructive, that is, their teaching causes factions and is divisive. They literally make up clever lies that Peter says, "turn against the master who bought them" (2 Peter 2:1). In other words Peter is saying, our sovereign God bought us with a price, that is the blood of Christ. We are no longer our own, we belong to God our master. However, false teaching denies that truth, and rather than adding to God's glory, they deny, at some level, God's right to be our sovereign Lord. Sometimes it is manifested in stories intended to impress us about the glory of their ministry or how they have a teaching that you will not find anywhere else.

Along with unorthodox teaching, Peter gives us a few other signs for a identifying false teachers. First is their shameful sexual ethics, meaning, they condone repeated acts of sexual immorality. To these teachers, sin and ethics are a matter of personal choice. Purity and obedience are replaced by self-fulfillment and self expression. Great popularity is sadly another hallmark of false teaching, as Peter writes "many will follow." While this is not a determining factor by itself it is often a key component with other signs. Finally, there is a de-emphasis on Christ along with impure motives. Christ's way is slandered or obscured and greed becomes the defining motive for such false teaching. This is entirely a man-centered religion instead of Christ-centered.

Much of the false teaching today has found its way into our gullible churches, through popular authors and personalities, who promote that organized religion only offers partial glimpses of God. Thus we need to seek an experience with God through feelings rather than dogma. Author Neil Donald Walsch in his popular book *Conversations With God* writes, "Listen to your feelings. Listen to your highest thoughts. Whenever any of these differ from what you've been told by teachers or read in books forget their words." [51]

The author, tells us that one day he simply started writing down his direct conversations with God. The God he speaks to is not Christian, nor identified with any other major religion. Walsch presents a God who satisfies the spiritual yearnings of our culture.

For other misguided teachers, sin, evil and hell are considered illusions that will ultimately be reconciled rather than overcome. Elizabeth Gilbert, the author of *Eat, Pray, Love,* assures readers that there is no such thing in this universe as hell except maybe in our own terrified minds. [52]

Peter tells us, when these false beliefs are smuggled into the church and begin to supersede the authority of God's word, there are some serious consequences ahead. "God condemned them long ago, and their destruction is on the way" (2 Peter 2:3b). Literally, this verse says their condemnation from long ago has not been idle and their destruction has not been sleeping. In other words, don't be fooled, God has not been dozing off and is fully aware how this undermines the gospel of truth.

To further make his point Peter gives three biblical examples of God's judgment in the Old Testament: fallen angels, a flooded world, (the story of Noah), and filthy cities, (the story of Sodom and Gomorrah). In the Greek these verses, four through nine, are one long sentence beginning with, "if God did not spare", and ending with "then." It's one of those if and then clauses of Scripture. It is not my intention to unpack these Old Testament stories in this book but let me summarize Peter's very ordered thoughts. His examples of God's judgment follow the chronology in Genesis and the stories gradually reduce in scale, from the cosmic angels, to the widespread flood of the earth, to the local cities of Sodom and Gomorrah. The angels sinned and are being held for judgment without exception. Noah's world was ungodly but he stood for righteousness, so those who believed him were protected. And the cities of Sodom and Gomorrah were more than just ungodly, they were wicked. Yet Lot is rescued because he was distressed by all the evil around him. So we have this one long sentence full of judgment and distraction as the result of false teaching, but it's also full of God's mercy.

Peter doesn't want us to be deceived by false teaching but he also doesn't want us to despair. The good news is that God is still in control. God is in control of both the godly and the ungodly. God marked out Noah and Lot as righteous and the other people were marked as ungodly. "So you see God knows how to rescue godly people from their trials, even while punishing the wicked right up until the day of judgment" (2 Peter 2:9). Peter's examples show us that God knows how to rescue the godly and punish the ungodly and as readers of his letter we are invited to put ourselves in the godly category. God knows how to rescue us from our trials, our tests of faith, and those internal struggles of doubt and unbelief. God knows how to rescue us from the temptations of compromising our faith, of conforming to what is popular, rather than what is truthful. He has provided all that is needed to see that we emerge with our faith intact.

But here is the important thing. The true heroes in Peter's examples, Noah and Lot, stand out against the prevailing unholy culture. That is not easy to do, especially when the ungodliness has infiltrated the church with its false teachings. Christians today will find it difficult and sometimes painful to be faithful to God's truth. God's provision for keeping us faithful will most assuredly involve enduring the trials of life. Those trials are especially hard to endure when it feels like God is no longer in control, when it seems like the ungodly and unfaithful are winning. That is when the false teaching, that puts more importance on feeling good then finding God, more emphasis on coming to God for what he can do for us then coming to God for who he is, that is when comfortable untruths become the greatest temptation for the church.

Our challenging culture is changing as churches are in decline and the bulk of a new generation is growing up outside of the Christian faith. People are turning to what some call "The Church of Oprah" or the church of whatever celebrity is popular in the moment. This has lead to a religious kind of therapy that seeks happiness over a relationship with a living God, leaving us with a new version of deism; a God who exists but is not very involved with our daily activities. The concepts of sin and obedience, an understanding of God's Kingdom and His grace, have been lost in this pursuit of a self-fulfilled life.

We are exposed to the voice of false teachers almost every day. If you watch any television, listen to any radio or podcasts, keep up on the news, or interact with just about anyone in modern society, you are being exposed to some form of false teaching. If you cannot identify any voices you hear as false, it's not because you aren't being exposed, but because you're falling for them in some way.

In the Disney animated classic Alice in Wonderland, Alice wanders through a frustrating world of tardy rabbits, singing flowers, and one curious talking cat. Her visit with the cat begins as she continues down a mysterious darkened trail and stops at a large tree. The tree is covered with signs that point in every possible direction: "Up," "Down," "Yonder," "Back," "This Way," and "That Way." Poor Alice looks more confused than ever and asks herself, "Now let's see. Where was I? I wonder which way I ought to go?" Just then, Alice hears a melodic voice that seems to be drifting down from the trees. She looks all around and finally observes two ghostly eyes and a wide toothy grin floating amongst the boughs of the great tree. The grinning teeth inquire of Alice, "Lose something?" "N-n-no, I was just" stammers Alice in reply. Suddenly, a pink-striped feline body emerges from the branches. "Oh, you're a cat!" "A cheshire cat," he responds.

"I just want to ask which way I ought to go," asks Alice. "Well that depends on where you want to get to," says the cat. "Well, it really doesn't matter," answers Alice. "Then it really doesn't matter which way you go," says the enigmatic cat just before vanishing into the woods again. [53]

Are too many of us so comfortable, and also confused about the truth, that we believe it doesn't really matter which way we go? But here is what Jesus said about that, "You can only enter God's kingdom through the narrow gate. The highway that leads to destruction is broad and it's gate is wide for the many who choose the easy way, but the gateway to life is small and the road is narrow and only a few ever find it" (John 7:13-14).

Probably the most popular criticism of Christianity today is that it is so narrow, and exclusive. To say Jesus is the only way is restrictive of our freedoms. Technically they are right. Truth by definition is narrow. It can also be hard. Falsehood is broad and easy but according to Jesus and Peter it also leads to destruction. Unlike Alice in Wonderland, if you have decided where you want to end up, it does matter which direction you go. And if that destination is a holy life in God's kingdom, then the way you should go is the way, the truth, and the life of Jesus Christ. It is not always comfortable and it is often challenging but Peter has assured us God knows how to rescue us from our trials, even from our struggles with doubt and unbelief that can tempt us to follow the world's comfortable falsehoods.

"The ultimate measure of a man is not where he stands
in moments of comfort and convenience, but where
he stands at times of challenge and controversy."
Martin Luther King Jr., *Leadership*, vol. 16, no. 3.

CHAPTER 6 - CHARACTER AND CONSEQUENCES OF FALSE TEACHING

I had the honor of joining Dr. Ray Bakke, Dr. Robert Lupton and several others on an urban consult in Pretoria, South Africa a few years after apartheid had been dismantled.

We were there to work with a ministry that was bringing churches together to help blacks and coloreds integrate into the new but still segregated South Africa. While we came to teach we learned far more than we taught, especially in our time with Desmond Tutu and the Truth and Reconciliation Commission. It was difficult to hear the admitted stories of murder by Afrikaner soldiers, but also glorious to hear about the gracious forgiveness offered by the victims' families. Even though South Africa was still a very divided nation, true biblical reconciliation was taking place. It was not at all comfortable for the violent perpetrators or the grieving victims to engage the consequences of the apartheid culture. But through the confession of guilt and the granting of forgiveness, a visible picture of God's Kingdom was discovered and the joy of that discovery was experienced. One such story involved a woman who not only forgave the man who was responsible for the murder of her husband and son, but actually went forward in the courtroom to physically embrace him. As she did the confessor slumped to the floor in her arms and the courtroom began a spontaneous chorus of "Amazing Grace".

The system of apartheid in South Africa, a sophisticated but oppressive structure of racism that reigned for decades, was based in large part on theological doctrines that were formed at Stellenbosch University in the 1930s and 1940s. The Afrikaner nationalism and distorted Christian theology that came from Stellenbosch's Seminary fueled many Afrikaner's belief that they were God's chosen people. They saw themselves as biologically superior to other races. Therefore, they felt called to create a new segregated society that would allow them to civilize other people while not tainting themselves with the "darkness and barbarism" of those inferior groups.

These doctrines gave the white South Africans religious justification for horrific crimes against their countrymen and women. More than 3.5 million black, Indian, and biracial people were removed from their homes in what was one of the largest mass removals in modern history. Nonwhite political representation was obliterated. Black South Africans were denied citizenship and relegated to the slums called "bantustans." The government segregated education, medical care, beaches, and other public services, providing black, Indian, and other "colored" people with significantly inferior services. The result was a segregated society where people were dehumanized based on beliefs that were supported by bad theology. [54] Even though apartheid had ended, the racist residue was still very evident during our monthlong visit. Gated white communities now had barbed wire on their walls, Black and white children were not allowed to sit together on school buses, and the greatest white fight ever took place in Johannesburg as Blacks came to the city looking for work. Racism and racial bigotry were alive and well.

While this may be an extreme example of the character and consequences of false teaching, it highlights the susceptibility of a faith that sought a comfortable homogeneous environment. It was a faith that was unwilling to engage a challenging culture and that saw itself as superior to other ethnic groups. Some believe we may be facing a similar, albeit for now, less severe challenge in our country today.

> Christian nationalism is an ideology that fuses
> Christians' love of God and country. It hinges on the
> narrative that the United States has a special covenant
> with the Christian God. This ideology has emerged at
> various times in U.S. history, but a distinct, aggres-
> sive iteration seems to have materialized today, ac-
> cording to a Think Progress report. This most recent
> version rejects secular society and seeks to restore
> America's identity as a Christian nation. [55]

It would certainly be a good thing for Americans to reflect the Christian values of Scripture, to love God and neighbors as ourselves, with shalom being our guide and goal. That happens when we "make the Kingdom of God our primary" (Matthew 6:33) and not idolizing America under the false assumption we are superior to all others as God's chosen nation. Such idol worship, as Tim Keller says, "means turning a good thing into an ultimate thing." [56] If we want security, possessions, success, popularity, or even a Christian nation, more than we want God Himself, we are missing the mark. False teaching most often focuses on the benefits of the Christian life rather than the source of the Christian life. It leads us away from a relationship with God and ultimately to an alternate or counterfeit god that may encourage our sense of superiority.

Such teaching that sees one group as superior over another ignores the character of God's impartiality (Deuteronomy 10:17) and Peter's revelation that "clearly God doesn't show partiality", as he entered a Gentile's house for the first time (Acts 10:34). It also misses Jesus' words and works of breaking down the "walls of hostility that used to separate us", ending a whole system of exclusion (Ephesians 2:14-15). That system had a series of walls in and around Jerusalem that literally excluded groups of people. The wall around the city kept out the lepers, who were considered unclean. That is why they could be seen begging for alms at the gates of Jerusalem, as they were not allowed in the city. As you went into the city and approached the temple there was another wall that excluded the Gentiles and further into the temple, a court and wall that excluded Jewish woman. The last wall, of course, was the curtain outside the holy of holies, where only the High Priest was allowed on the Day of Atonement to make sacrifices for the sins of the people. We know that it was on the cross that Jesus removed those barriers of exclusion, but Matthew reveals that Jesus also addressed them in his earthly ministry.

In Matthew chapters five through seven, the Apostle gives us a picture of the ethics of the coming Kingdom in Jesus' Sermon on the Mount and then in chapters eight and nine, he shows Jesus demonstrating the Kingdom with ten miracles. The teaching Messiah becomes the touching Messiah. In the first three touching miracles Matthew's gospel records, Jesus heals a leper, a Centurion's son, and then Peter's mother-in-law. Down come the walls of exclusion for the outsiders, those considered inferior, the lepers, the Gentiles and women. When Jesus goes to the cross, the final wall of exclusion, the curtain is torn from top to bottom allowing all who put their faith in Jesus Christ to enter into the holy of holies. Black and white, rich and poor, male and female, democrat and republican, citizens and immigrants are all welcome to enter the Kingdom through grace by faith in Christ, because God shows no favoritism. Whether the Pharisees of Jesus' day, the extreme exclusionists of our culture, or the subtle prejudice and preferences of our peer group, they are all examples of influential teachings that contradict the truth of God's character and Christ's gospel. [57]

Peter gives us a picture of such misleading instructors, a sketch of the "character and consequences of false teachers" (2 Peter 2:10-22). The old proverb that a picture is worth a thousand words applies here, because false teaching is most often revealed in false living. Jesus in His Sermon on the Mount warns about false prophets saying, "You can detect them by the way they act just as you can identify a tree by it's fruit" (Matthew 7:16). Our tendency at this point is to immediately think of the obvious charlatans and cult leaders of our day, but false teachers come in all shapes, sizes, and subtleties. They may be in our church pulpits, but more often they come from our cultural icons.

Thus Peter starts with the character of false teachers representing again our world's triune gods of money, sex and power. False teachers desire to make money, "They train themselves to be greedy" (2 Peter 3:14). The word "train" in the Greek is gymnazo, where we get our word gymnasium. They worked hard at being greedy and were experts in teaching others to be greedy. Peter also says they followed the way of Balaam. Balaam was a prophet who was offered money to curse Israel (Numbers 22). But as he was on his way to make his money, God spoke to him through his donkey. That got his attention and he went on to speak only what God wanted him to speak. It is always God's word that provides the correction for the temptation of following the untruths of greed.

In the movie *Wall Street*, Gordon Gecko is a business tycoon bent on success at any price. During his takeover bid at a paper company's stockholder meeting, he lays out his perspective. "The point is, ladies and gentlemen, is that greed, for lack of a better word, is good. Greed is right. Greed works." [58] Unfortunately, in many circles that is still the prevailing motto, albeit a false one. And here is the thing about greed; it's hard to detect in ourselves. As a pastor I have had people come to me and confess that they struggle with almost every kind of sin. However, I don't remember anyone ever coming to me and saying, "I spend too much money on myself. I think my lust for money is hurting my family, my soul, and others." Greed hides itself from the victim. The idol of money in the sin of greed blinds our own heart. Greed is easy to identify in the false teaching of someone who wants your money to buy himself a new multi-million dollar jet, but harder to see in ourselves.

False teachers also delight in sensual pleasures. Pleasure here is where we get our word hedonism, a significant characterization of our culture today, seeking more and more pleasure, a lust that is never satisfied. Pleasure is a goal that can never be reached. The false teachers of Peter's day not only lived for pleasure but promoted the search for it. They seduced and lured unstable people into sin, while they committed adultery with their eyes. Internet porn has come a long way from the days of *Playboy* magazine in teaching and seducing men to view women as sexual objects. However, women are catching up and being taught to look at men in the same way.

In 2012, the New York Times reported on a conference of female missionaries (a term the article used) who are intent on changing the world. The women who gathered in Madrid came from numerous countries, to participate in the biennial Cosmic Conference to promote the values of the bestselling magazine in America: *Cosmopolitan*. According to the article, these Cosmo missionaries were intent on spreading the good news of Cosmo, which is summed up in their motto: fun, fearless, female! Under the direction of the US editor Kate White, Cosmo strives to offer serious advice to women around the world on matters of beauty, relationships, careers, and sex- especially sex. The New York Times article reported: its covers rarely fail to feature at least one bold, all caps rendering of the word sex. A sampling of the 2012 headlines includes, "50 Sex Tips," "99 Sex Questions" and "His Best Sex Ever." Through their 64 international editions, the magazine now spreads wild sex stories to 100 million teens and young women in more than 100 nations, including a few countries where any discussion of sex is taboo. Kate White admits that some people might object to Cosmo's obsession with sexual topics, but she's unabashedly proud of how that focus sets the magazine apart from her competitors. White said, "Every Cosmo reader expects to have herself and her pleasures taken care of, equally. We reinforce the idea all the time that, yes, we want you to be a fabulous lover, we want to give you those skills, but you better get it back, baby, because that's what you deserve." [59]

Lastly these false teachers despised any kind of authority. They were so prideful and arrogant, they scoffed or mocked the power of fallen angels, and ridiculed the idea of Satan and demonic powers. Peter tells us that even the good angels respected demonic influence. Now Christ has disarmed these powers and authorities but we dare not minimize the danger of their influence. Christians cannot be possessed by demons but we can be led astray, especially if we have set up idols in our hearts and have unrepentant sin or unforgiveness in our heart. Anytime we pretend that sin is not really sin we can open ourselves up to demonic influences. These false teachers were so full of ego they did not believe in this kind of power. They only believed in their own powerful ability that worked at making life more pleasurable and the gospel more comfortable. There are still teachers today who use their position of authority to discard inconvenient biblical truths in order to refute any future judgment based on a perceived set of moral absolutes.

So the character of false teachers are: desiring to make money; delighting in pleasures; and despising authority through their greed, sensuality, and arrogance. These character traits also have their consequences (2 Peter 2:17-22). First, non-Christians are deceived into rejecting God's truth. Peter gives two metaphors for these teachers' negative impact: dried-up springs of water and clouds blown away by the wind. Both are pictures of deception, of empty promises. In the dry climate of the Ancient Near East, springs of water were a blessing for the weary traveler, sometimes even lifesaving. Imagine the disappointment to find a dried-up spring when you are dying of thirst. It's the same with the picture of a cloud that holds the promise of rain but then disappears when the wind blows. False teachers were and are impressive on the outside but hollow and empty on the inside. They were luring people who had come to seek something about Jesus back into sin, through the promise of freedom, but it was all an illusion. These teachers had bought a closet full of expensive suits, learned to speak with great rhetorical flare, had rented a big arena, and charged admission. However, the well was dry, the message was empty, the Spirit was missing, but a good time was had by all. The result was that people rejected the real truth about God for some great entertainment and ended up worse off than they were before. "They make these Proverbs come true: 'a dog returns to its vomit' and 'a washed pig returns to the mud'" (2 Peter2:22). The people had started to get cleaned up but ended back in the mud and returning to the vomit. Their sinful self-indulgence is compared to vomit and mud, a vivid picture of the consequences of false teachers.

While non-Christians are deceived into rejecting God's truth, Christians can be deceived into cheapening God's grace. False teaching entices us to take advantage of God's grace with that same promise of freedom. "They promise freedom, but they themselves are slaves to sin and corruption. For you are a slave to whatever controls you" (2 Peter 2:19). They were teaching that you can decide for yourselves what is right or wrong even while they were really enslaved to sin. That is not freedom. The gospel gives us great assurance that we are secured in our salvation, secured in our position with God. John writes this in his gospel, "My sheep recognize my voice; I know them, and they follow me. I give them eternal life, and they will never perish. No one will snatch them away from me, for my Father has given them to me, and he is more powerful than anyone else. So no one can take them away from me" (John 10:27-29).

This does not mean we can now do whatever we want. Cheap grace is too prevalent in the church today. There is limited accountability for our sin and little regard for God's holiness. Our desire for that kind of freedom, doing whatever we want or freedom from God's truth, only leaves us enslaved to sin. However, true freedom from sin leads to a joyful slavery to God and a life of holiness.

When I was a young boy, friends and I attempted to ride our bikes down a very steep dirt road that had a 90° turn halfway down. Our goal was to see if we could ride all the way down through the curve without applying our breaks. I chickened out, I hit my brakes as I entered the sharp bend. A couple of my friends were brave enough to keep their feet from touching the brakes, but then losing control in the loose gravel. Instead of the exhilarating freedom of a highspeed bike ride, there was the pain of bruised and bloody knees and elbows. You see true freedom is found only in a committed relationship to a God who knows how to maximize our fun while applying the appropriate brakes to our lives.

As already mentioned, one of the biggest idols of our present culture is individualism, the absolute right and freedom to choose the life we want to live. The only thing considered wrong in this idol worship, is to keep other individuals from living the way they choose. That means there is no moral authority higher than the happiness of self. This is the man-centered focus Peter has been warning about. Yet another false teaching that has crept into the church. Our worship of individualism has caused us to become dupes of media, entertainment and marketing. These are some of the most influential false teachers of our day. Advertisers have shifted from telling us the benefits of products to promoting a story that promises us a heightened image and an exceptional life. Nicholas Wolterstorff in his book, *Justice: Rights and Wrongs,* points out that our culture today defines the happy life as full of experiential pleasures, where as in biblical times a happy life meant a life that is lived well, with character, courage, humility, love and justice. [60] This narrative from the media and marketing today is a false gospel, a story that rejects spiritual authority for the autonomy of the individual. They promote sensual pleasures and greed but in the end it is a worldview that is as useless as dried-up springs of water.

So if individualism is the idol that we worship and marketing is the gospel that enhances our image, then work now becomes a form of salvation, whereby we can buy the products that promise a life of happiness and success. In this process relationships can become pawns in our quest for the Holy Grail and we can easily begin to believe the falsehood that we are superior to others. This is one of the significant untruths in our culture, a man-centered gospel that has seeped into the church. It contributes to the sacred and secular divide, as well as keeping us from integrating our faith into all of life. Our vocations become just a means to an end rather than God's intended mission field. It is a false gospel that keeps us from seeing the purpose of the church, the importance of the Sabbath, and the significance of our mission in the world. Let's be honest for most of us a pastor gets about 70 minutes a month to present us with the true gospel story, so our life can reflect that narrative. It is not enough. Not when we are bombarded with another gospel day in and day out. We need to honor the Sabbath but we also need to be in God's word every day. We need the truth to grow as Christians but just as importantly, others need to see and hear God's living story demonstrated and proclaimed in our lives.

It is understandable why so many of us Christians settle for the comfortable life that this false gospel provides. It gives us an aura of Christianity while pursuing a life of success and happiness. It is also safer in light of the harmful rhetoric that shoots from the various cultural bunkers, aimed at quickly attaching a complete identity to those perceived as having a different worldview. A comment favoring a democratic policy, labels one as a leftist liberal, and support for free markets makes you a right-wing conservative. Similar theological labeling happens just as quickly in the church today.

On the Sunday after the 2008 election, I made an apolitical remark on the historical nature of our first Black President, since half our congregation were African Americans. Monday morning I received a scathing email from a young couple, who I had counseled and married a few years earlier. They were outraged that I had evidently become pro abortion by even mentioning our new president's name. I quickly invited them to sit down with me and our three Black elders so we could listen to each other and come to an understanding. The meeting was gracious and it was clearly established that the church's theological position was pro life, but the young couple's ideology was so deep and with the superiority they felt in their position, they left the church that week.

These kind of fruitless encounters have only increased today. The old adage against ever discussing politics or religion in public has taken on a new significance. However, what remains are the extreme sides of left and right, shouting at each other from their respective theological and ideological foxholes. It is into this challenging culture that God is calling His church to engage and in the process it can become a purifying trial. There is a huge void between the left and right that provides an opportunity for the gospel of God's Kingdom to be presented as the truthful alternative. It calls for bold but gracious conversations with deeply entrenched and sometimes false perspectives. It requires what Miroslav Volf calls "double vision." Volf says we must allow others and those we are in conflict with to "readjust our perspective as we take into account their perspective." [61] This takes great humility, as it requires the recognition we have not always cornered the market on truth. Double vision involves a self-giving love whose "weakness is stronger than social concern and foolishness is wiser than rational thought." [62] This ministry engagement rarely produces the results we think our efforts deserve. That was the great scandal of the cross as both God and those Jesus ministered to abandoned Him. The real results are the joy and healing found in the embrace of the other regardless of their appreciative response. This reversal of perspectives is what keeps us from perverting justice or what Amos calls "turning justice into poison" (Amos 6:12). This double vision must especially be applied in the church.

The Apostle Paul wrote, "So we have stopped evaluating others by what the world thinks about them" (2 Corinthians 5:16). It seems that the most powerful four-letter word today is "them" – them other folks who are different than us. Those who are different in race, ethnicity, politics, religion, sex, or whose views are different than ours. Much of our identity, community and power are established by the measurement of our differences from "them." The church at Corinth had become seers instead of believers, they were seeing others from a human point of view. They were measuring "them" based on the distinctions of their world – male and female, Jew and Greek, slave and free. Paul writes "that those who become Christians become new persons. They are not the same anymore, for the old life is gone. A new life has begun!" (2 Corinthians 5:17). This new humanity was only made possible by the grace of a God who shows no partiality and the blood of His Son, who hung out with women, Samaritans, lepers, tax collectors and an assortment of sinners. When we bring our measuring sticks to church and ask God to bless them we nullify God's grace. No wonder so much of the unbelieving world has stopped responding to us. Instead we should bring our dueling yardsticks to the cross and ask God to crucify them. From the world's point of view life is about control but at the cross we surrender our control, especially our control over the measurement of others. The way out of the garden of evaluating others by what the world thinks about them and into the new humanity of God's kingdom, is surrendering our measurements of others.

Reportedly, President Lyndon B. Johnson said to a young Bill Moyers: "If you can convince the lowest white man he's better than the best colored man, he won't notice you're picking his pocket. Hell, give him somebody to look down on, and he'll empty his pockets for you." [63] Whether from a subtle Christian Nationalism or the worship of individualism, fueled by greed, sensuality and arrogance, there is an influential false teaching today that tempts us to feel superior over others different than us and undermines the gospel of grace.

The Apostle Paul taught a different worldview to follow; that in humility we are to count others as more significant than ourselves (Philippians 2:3). Even those who are uneducated or jobless, too different or too disagreeable, are to be counted not just as equals but as more significant than us. This is the exact opposite of feeling superior. Paul's point is not about what others are but what we count others to be. The focus is not on how well they read or how much money they make, the color of their skin or their political views. The focus is: Will we count them as worthy of our friendship, help or encouragement? Will we take thought not just for our interests but for theirs? Will we encourage them, take the time to get to know them, help and build them up? How does this other-oriented, coming together from divergent directions, happen? It comes from the same humility just mentioned with Volf's double vision. A humility that comes from recognizing the overwhelming, moment by moment act of God's grace in our lives, promised for eternity. Imagine how different our world could be if we actually counted others as more significant. Maybe a more civil political discourse, a less segregated Sunday morning church, a little less racism and classism; just imagine the possibilities. God did imagine it, that is why He sent his Son to establish His Kingdom, a new way to live in harmony, by loving God and loving our neighbors as ourselves. Doing this is hard and it is rarely comfortable but it is God's designed plan where He purifies our faith and makes the joy of His kingdom visible.

PART 3 - HOPE IN CHRIST

"Though Jesus cast a vision for a better kingdom now and in the future, as long as it is Saturday, the fulfillment of that vision still awaits until Sunday dawns." Philip Yancey, *The Jesus I Never Knew*.

CHAPTER 7 - RECAPTURING GOD'S COMING KINGDOM

There are two ways of handling pressure. One is illustrated by a bathysphere, the miniature submarine used to explore the ocean in places so deep that the water pressure would crush a conventional submarine like an aluminum can. Bathyspheres compensate with plate steel several inches thick, which keeps the water out but also makes them heavy and hard to maneuver. Inside they are cramped. When these craft descend to the ocean floor, however, they find they are not alone. When their lights are turned on and you look through the tiny, thick plate glass windows, you begin to see fish. Fish represent a second method of coping with extreme pressure but in an entirely different way. They don't build thick skins; they remain supple and free. They compensate for the outside pressure through equal and opposite pressure inside themselves. Christians, likewise, don't half to be hard and thick skinned, as long as they appropriate God's power within to equal the pressure without. We don't have to withdraw into the thick walls of a church to withstand the cultural challenges today. As Peter taught in his first chapter, the church has the power and promises of Christ to overcome the temptation to either escape from or conform to the world around it.

This is the hope Peter wants us to have in the midst of pressures resulting from our lazy faith and the lure of false teachings. The apostle says he wants to "stimulate our wholesome thinking" (2 Peter 3:1), he wants to stir up pure thoughts. Eugene Peterson in his *Message* paraphrase says, Peter wants to "hold our minds in a state of undistracted attention." This is more than a mental exercise, it involves the ability to discern spiritual truth and apply it to our lives. It offers great hope for our Monday morning mission in a world without a lot of truth. Wholesome here means fruitful and productive, in other words it will pass the full test of being examined under light. There will be fruitful and productive actions behind stimulated and wholesome thinking. In the urban vernacular we would say it means "walking the talk."

In 1992, when we began to plant a church in an urban neighborhood of Pittsburgh, we had two seminary students go door to door with a set of questions to get to know the perceived needs of our neighbors. The last question asked what would they want to say to a new church and pastor in their neighborhood. One particular resident summed up the answer for all the other 59 questioned: "walk the talk." In other words, live out what you say you believe, be the same person you proclaim to be on Sunday when you walk around this neighborhood.

Tomato growers in central California are more successful at growing tomatoes than the tomato growers of all human history, they grew more tomatoes per acre than anyone ever had. But they did have one problem. That was to get their tomatoes into the salad bowls of Chicago and the fruit baskets of the Bronx unbruised, because a magnificent bruised tomato, in the hands of the tomato squeezers of the world, is only a bruised tomato. So they set agrotechnology to work and accomplished two marvelous things. First, they got a machine to pick the tomatoes while they were still yellow but very firm. Then they put the tomatoes on an assembly belt, passed them under a certain kind of light for seven seconds, and they came out a rosy red--a rosy pink, almost red. And then they devised a packaging such that you could put a bunch of tomatoes in a styrofoam crate, and lift it twenty feet high above solid concrete, and also take a bumper from a Chevy pickup, lift it twenty feet high above solid concrete, drop them both, and the bumper would come off worse than any one of those tomatoes. Agrotechnology wins again. But they had one problem: The tomato that the chef sliced into his salad in Chicago and the woman bought from the market in Boston didn't taste the way a tomato was supposed to taste. They had achieved enormous success at the means, but forgot the point and purpose, the end of it all. [64]

Too many churches and teachers have forgotten the point and purpose of the gospel. It is to make disciples, transforming lives into the image of Christ. The gospel prepares us to participate in God's redemptive work in all of the world, making God's kingdom visible. Instead much focus has been put on the, albeit well intended, means rather than the goal and it has pulled some into false teaching and a complacent Christianity. Focusing on the means produces a comfortable faith rather than growing disciples. Too much emphasis on the means attracts an audience but misses the goal of the gospel.

GK Chesterton wrote, "We do not want, as the newspapers say, a church that will move with the world. We want a church that will move the world." [65] There is a difference between a church and an audience. An audience is a group of unrelated people drawn together by a short-lived attraction. A church, on the other hand, is a family of God, a fellowship of Christ followers, a Spirit filled body, gathered together, then sent out on God's mission to "move the world."

That is why Peter calls us to "remember and understand what the prophets and apostles said and commanded" (2 Peter 3:2). Peter uses the word "commanded" in the singular form and thus is referring to the general demand that all believers conform to the image and mission of Christ - not falling prey to false teaching that would neglect a life of holiness or be distracted from our mission. In other words, Peter is saying believe rightly in order to behave rightly. This is in contrast to the false teachers who behaved wrongly and in the process made their wrong beliefs evident. Right beliefs leading to right behavior only comes from seeking the truth of God's word. That is why Peter wants to stimulate our wholesome thinking and refresh our memory.

Next Peter reminds us there will be scoffers in the last days, from Jesus' first coming until his second coming. They will laugh at the idea that there is a right belief that leads to right behavior. Scoffers to-day would say there are many acceptable beliefs that can lead to many acceptable behaviors. The many acceptable behaviors we call relativism and the many acceptable beliefs we call pluralism. Relativism is the idea that there are no moral truths and therefore many behaviors are acceptable. Pluralism is a social agreement that says people with different beliefs have a right to express them. Both, however, are based on the idea that there are no absolute truths. Peter gives us an example of this argument in 2 Peter 3:4. "This will be their argument; Jesus promised to come back. Did he? Then where is he? Why, as far back as anyone can remember, everything has remained exactly the same since the world was first created."

People were struggling with the delay of Christ's return. We are supposed to believe, they say, well Christ said he would return and he hasn't. Nothing has changed since he left, in other words, Jesus has made no difference in the world. Thus the world must be a closed system and God, if he exists at all, remains uninvolved. This is very similar to what skeptics say today. Part of what can contribute to our doubts and complacency in the Christian life, is the growing sense of unbelief in our world. We're surrounded by religious pluralism, the many different belief systems that exist, and some who outwardly scoff at Christianity. Yet as David Wells reminds us this is not a new thing.

> While religious pluralism may be a novel experience for us, it is putting us in touch with the world that surrounded the biblical authors. The pluralism and the paganism of our time were the common experience of the prophets and apostles. In Mesopotamia, there were thousands of gods and goddesses, many of which were known to the Israelites--indeed, sometimes known too well. ... Nothing, therefore, could be more remarkable than to hear the contention, even

from those within the Church, that the existence of religious pluralism today makes belief in the uniqueness of Christianity quite impossible. Had this been the necessary consequence of encountering a multitude of other religions, Moses, Isaiah, Jesus, and Paul would have given up biblical faith long before it became fashionable ... to do so. [66]

New Testament scholar and historian, Larry Hurtado, in his little book, *Why On Earth Did Anybody Become a Christian in the First Three Centuries?*, confirms Well's point. The New Testament world was very pluralistic. Everybody had their own gods and everybody had to accept everybody else's god. Even though Jews and Christians claimed their God was the only god, that was generally accepted because they were seen as ethnic groups. Their social and political persecution came, not as much from their religious belief system, but more as a result of false rumors concerning their involvement in cannibalism and promiscuous sex, as well as a subversive political view against Rome. However, many early historians, such as Justin, came to the defense of Christians and to debunk the falsehoods about their lifestyle. [67] The point Wells and Hurtado are making, is in the words of Solomon, "there is nothing new under the sun" (Ecclesiastes 1:9), and the challenging culture we face today is what Peter was addressing to his readers. The Apostle shows this flaw in the world's pluralistic reasoning from three biblical examples.

His first example is from creation. "They deliberately forget that God made the heavens by the word of his command and he brought the earth up from the water and surrounded it with water" (2 Peter 3:5). God literally spoke creation in to existence. He said, "Let there be light and there was light" (Genesis 1:3). John's gospel tells us that the word God spoke at creation was Jesus. "In the beginning the word already existed. He was with God, and he was God.....He created everything there is.....So the word became human and lived here on earth among us" (John 1:1,3,14). Peter's point is that the very continuance of our world points to the dependability of God's word. By God's word we exist. "By faith we understand that the entire universe was formed at God's. command, that what we now see did not come from anything that can be seen"(Hebrews 11:3). Peter is teaching that the creation story in Genesis 1 reveals that God's means of creation was his word and the agent of creation was the water. The results were the heaven and the earth. The false teachers had forgotten this and Peter calls us to remember it.

The second example Peter uses to refute the pluralistic scoffers and false teachers is the flood. "Then he used the water to destroy the world with a mighty flood" (2 Peter 3:6). The water was used in God's creation and now it is used in God's judgment. You see, every thing did not go on as it had from the beginning of creation. The same water and word God used to create, God also used to destroy. Peter refutes the false teachings that God has never intervened in history. He agrees with the stability of God's creative word but is showing that God's judicial word does intervene and gets involved in the unfolding history of our world.

Lastly, the same word of God tells us there is a future and a final judgment coming, although God's word has also delayed that judgment. "And God has also commanded that the heavens and the earth will be consumed by fire on the day of judgment, when ungodly people will perish" (2 Peter 3:7). What was destroyed at the flood was the human world. What lies in the future judgment is the fate of the whole creation, the heavens and earth. The flood was an advance warning of what will happen, a picture painted on a small canvas compared to what God has in store for his creation. Peter is defending God's word, God's truth, and God's very character. The fact that we do not see God actively judging his world is not a sign of his non-existence or his weakness. God is absolutely in control and his powerful and truthful word is being exercised by keeping his creation for its final judgment, when the present physical reality of all we see will be gloriously renewed with a new heaven and a new earth.

These three biblical examples argue against the false teacher's notion that "everything goes on as it has since the beginning of creation." Their implication was that God is not involved in the events of history. It's similar to the prevailing assumption today, rooted in the theory of evolution. Evolution dismisses any idea of a personal God intervening in the course of history. It assumes that our world operates through blind chance or at best some invariable laws of nature. With this prevailing worldview and with a lazy faith, we can easily succumb to this reigning assumption that we live in a closed universe with little or no room for God to act or reveal himself.

Dr. Jerome Frank at John's Hopkins talks about our "assumptive world." What he means is that all of us make assumptions about life, about God, about ourselves, about others, and about the way things are. He goes on to argue that when our assumptions are true to reality, we live relatively happy, well-adjusted lives. But when our assumptions are distant from reality, we become confused and angry and disillusioned. [68] So if in our assumptive world we embrace a theory of evolution, but then our world doesn't evolve into a nice orderly pattern we become disillusioned. On the other hand if our biblical worldview assumes God will quickly bring justice and judge those who do evil, or that God will bless us for our work with the oppressed, we also become disillusioned when his justice and our blessings are delayed. Our assumptions must be rooted in God's truth and our realities must be interpreted through God's word. So we guard against the temptation to think we can know precisely what God is doing in the events of our world. Earthquakes are not God's judgment against a specific sin and an economic up turn is not God's grace for those with a specific political view. A true biblical worldview affirms that God is active in the events of our lives. He has not stepped aside to let our lives take their own course. We may not know the significance or the specifics of God's involvement, but the hope for growing Christians in our challenging culture, is that our lives are filled with the presence and activity of a personal, holy and loving God, who is guiding us and his creation to a glorious and purposeful end.

This challenging culture in which we live is full of competing ideas and worldviews. In such a globalized and interconnected world, Christians are more than ever exposed to and influenced by varying views of reality and truth. Barna's research shows that only 17 percent of Christians who consider their faith important and attend church regularly actually have a biblical worldview. [69] Thus the challenge with these competing world views is that they contain threads of recognizable truth that Christians embrace without realizing their unbiblical distortions. For example, another Barna study found that 52 percent of practicing Christians strongly agree that the Bible teaches "God helps those who help themselves." [70] A quote made popular by Benjamin Franklin in *Poor Richard's Almanac,* but lacking any true biblical reference. Again, this is why Peter began chapter three with "I have tried to stimulate your wholesome thinking and refresh your memory." Peter wants to help his readers move from a comfortable faith, reinforced by unbiblical teaching, to recapturing a faith that reflects the holiness of God's coming Kingdom.

D. Lloyd Jones writes, as he finishes his sermon on this text, "God grant that our minds may thus be pure, and utterly free from all modern suggestions and teachings which would have us reject the clear teaching of the revelation of God in His Holy Word." [71]

"God's Kingdom is built not on perpetual motion, one-liners, and flashbulbs, but on Christ."
Carl F. H. Henry, *Money in Christian History, Christian History*, no. 14.

CHAPTER 8 - LOOKING FOR GOD'S COMING KINGDOM

When a discussion of the end times comes up we often have a mix of joy, uncertainty and for some even fear. Christ tells us no one knows the exact time of his return and thus the end of the world as we know it. I wonder if this lack of knowledge concerning dates and times is what really troubles us or is it the idea of a final judgment. What will it be like to stand in front of Christ and give an account for our lives? Author and pastor Frederick Buechner offers words that give the reality of that coming judgment, but at the same time gives the hope of a grace-filled love.

> The New Testament proclaims that at some unfore-seeable time in the future, God will ring down the final curtain on history, and there will come a Day on which all our days and all the judgments upon us and all our judgments upon each other will themselves be judged. The judge will be Christ. In other words, the one who judges us most finally will be the one who loves us most fully. [72]

There are many different views of what the end of the world will be like and even a few still believe there is never going to be an end. Some speak about an environmental apocalypse due to rising temperatures, melting glaciers, and shrinking ozone layers. Others follow a popular series of books that describe people disappearing from planes and a one-world government. Second Peter gives us a picture that is much simpler in chapter 3:8-13. Jesus will come again, the ungodly will be destroyed, the earth will be remade, giving us a new heaven and a new earth. The world as we know it will get a complete make over and the Kingdom of God will have fully come. Things will finally be as God intended from the beginning of creation. Peter also tells us, "You should look forward to that day and hurry it along" (2 Peter 3:12).

This is the continued hope Peter offers in his letter. After reminding his readers of the truth of the gospel in chapter one and then warning us about the consequences of false teaching and an uncommitted faith in chapter two, the Apostle provides hope. If the possibility of some future cosmic destruction is true, what encouragement can we find for our future and how can we possibly influence its coming? Three times Peter encourages the reader to look forward, beyond the end of this world, to a new reality. Peter writes, "Everything around us is going to melt away" (2 Peter 3:12b), referring to the destructive fire in the previous verses. The present participle of "going to melt away" in the original text indicates that this process has already started. [73] While most of today's scientists believe there is an environmental catastrophe in our future, the Apostle acknowledged it has already started. The difference is Peter sees this end as an encounter with the living Christ not as an impersonal and gradual disappearance of the world as we know it. If this is the case, Peter then asks a rhetorical question as to what sort of lives should Christians be living? Holy and godly lives is his answer.

Peter's answer also addresses the question of how can we, as ordinary Christians, hurry the coming of Christ and the end of the world? Peter previously wrote in verse eight and nine that Jesus is not being slow in his promise to return but rather he is being patient to give time for everyone to repent. If God is delaying the return of His Son because of sin, then we may encourage his return by our holy and godly lives, living lives of repentance and faith. Whenever we pray "Thy

Kingdom come," we are asking God to hasten that reality, but we are also making a commitment to live as loyal and obedient citizens of his Kingdom. Peter is emphasizing that Jesus is coming back, his Kingdom is coming, whether we believe it or not, so start looking and living for it now.

Yet, just as in Peter's time, there are "scoffers" today "who will laugh at the truth and do every evil thing they desire" (2 Peter 3:3). The arguments today are possibly the same. Nothing has happened to make us think Christ is returning. For the original readers of Peter's letter it had been 30 years since Jesus left so why hasn't He returned? Some of the apostles had died and Peter himself was near death when he wrote this letter. Nothing is happening, there is no sign of Christ returning, and the miracles of the early church are diminishing. The church was starting to believe there is no second coming of Christ.

However, it wasn't just what was not happening around them that contributed to their doubt of Christ's return. As mentioned in my previous chapter Peter wrote, "They deliberately forget that God made the heavens by the word of his command....Then he used the water to destroy the world with a mighty flood" (2 Peter 3:5-6). This is not the first time Peter has challenged the people with their willful forgetfulness. Their complacency and the effort of false teachers have encouraged this intentional lack of memory. If God's word can create and destroy, it can certainly bring about Christ's return, bring an end to all we see and birth a new heaven and a new earth. Peter confronts his readers, then and today, who think there is never going to be a final accounting for our lives or an end to our world. "You must not forget", Peter writes (2 Peter 3:8).

Peter has already established that the delay of Christ's return does not mean it is not going to happen. It means God is giving everyone more time, but with that time they must overcome their willful forgetfulness. In my years of doing pastoral counseling, I learned it was sometimes helpful to ask the question, "What are you refusing to look at in your life, what are you pretending does not exist in your life?" I think it may be a similar question Peter is addressing. We can believe whatever we want about a final judgment or the end of the world, but the idea that there is not going to be such an event, may be coming from a desire to live however we want and that there will never be any accountability for our selfish actions. An admission to the contrary could interrupt our devotion to the things of this world. Peter's teaching, however, is making it abundantly clear that this world, which we may love more than God's Kingdom, is going to burn. Our comfortable life devoted to the pleasure of sex, the accumulation of wealth, or the pursuit of power is going to disappear.

The false teachers in Peter's letter "trained themselves to be greedy", (vs. 2:14), "despised authority", (vs. 2:10), and gave themselves over to "shameful immorality",

(vs. 2:2). This is all going to melt away in the fire of judgment. Peter implies that the only thing that will survive the scrutiny of God's judgment is the fruitful obedience of our holy and godly lives. In his book, *The Wounded Healer*, Henri Nouwen retells a tale from ancient India.

> Four royal brothers decided each to master a special ability. Time went by, and the brothers met to reveal what they had learned.
>
> 'I have mastered a science,' said the first, 'by which I can take but a bone of some creature and create the flesh that goes with it.'
>
> 'I,' said the second, 'know how to grow that creature's skin and hair if there is flesh on its bones.'
>
> The third said, 'I am able to create its limbs if I have the flesh, the skin, and the hair.'
>
> 'And I,' concluded the fourth, 'know how to give life to that creature if its form is complete.'
>
> Thereupon the brothers went into the jungle to find a bone so they could demonstrate their specialties. As

fate would have it, the bone they found was a lion's. One added flesh to the bone, the second grew hide and hair, the third completed it with matching limbs, and the fourth gave the lion life. Shaking its mane, the ferocious beast arose and jumped on his creators. He killed them all and vanished contentedly into the jungle. [74]

We also can pursue and create what can devour us. Goals and dreams can be a good thing but they can consume us. Possessions and power can turn and destroy us, unless we first seek God's kingdom and his righteousness (Matthew 6:33). Peter emphasizes that this coming Kingdom will be a place where righteousness reigns, "a world where everyone is right with God" (2 Peter 3:13). Therefore we must allow God to form and shape all that we do and make in this life, so it remains an expression of his holiness.

There is an additional reason that readers of this letter may struggle with the truth of the end times and God's final judgment. We don't like to think about God destroying ungodly people. Certainly the unbelieving world, who holds up tolerance as a supreme value, does not like the idea that some people are in and some people are out. Who could serve such an arbitrary God? Even though we read of God's patience to give people time to repent, this theme of death and destruction for the unrepentant is also distasteful for some Christians. We want a loving God who will provide his saving grace to everyone. On the other hand, God's patience can also be seen by some as God's absence when the world seems out of control. Where is God when innocent people are being killed, children are abused, and whole nations are going hungry? It appears God can appear too severe to some and too patient for others. How difficult it is sometimes for God to please us when our faith is centered on our desires. Regardless of our leanings we must not allow them to matriculate into unbelief. That was the error of the false teachers who argued against any final judgment of God. Peter's conviction is that based on God's holiness he has a responsibility to judge and out of his love he offers a gracious salvation, including giving more time for unbelievers to repent.

What is our reluctance to fully embrace the truth of Peter's teaching on the end times and God's impending judgment? A group of Americans were surveyed concerning issues of life after death and only forty-eight percent believe we go to heaven or hell, depending on confession of sins and accepting Jesus. [75] Are we like Demas, who Paul writes had deserted him because he loved the things of the world (2 Timothy 4:10)? Are we too focused on what we might lose in this present age instead of what we gain in God's promise, the promise of a new heaven and a new earth, where we are in a right relationship with God? Lloyd Jones affirms this when he says, "We have been so concerned about the state of affairs here on earth that we have forgotten the glory which is to come."[76] Until we submit to Peter's exhortation to look forward to that day and even hurry it along, it will be difficult to live holy and godly lives. Maybe we lack a fuller biblical understanding of God's coming Kingdom.

Geerhardus Vos wrote a book entitled, *The Teaching of Jesus Concerning the Kingdom of God and the Church.* In his final chapter he writes that the Kingdom of God "means the renewal of the world through the introduction of supernatural forces." [77] For Vos the Kingdom is not some academic head knowledge or an emotional experience of the heart but the power and presence of God coming into the world. It is an entrance that brings about objective changes, overcoming sin and suffering. Vos sees three important realms of the Kingdom that cannot be separated. The first is God's saving grace that provides our entrance into the already and not yet of God's Kingdom, as well as the promised fulfillment of that reality. Second is the realm of righteousness that Peter refers to, where every one is in a right relationship with God. Vos emphasizes that this is a new way of living in relationship with others and the world around us that reflects the King's new standards. Thirdly is the realm of joy, available to us now as God's power renews all of creation and culture. Vos believes that these realms of the Kingdom are manifested in the church as she gathers and through Christians as we are sent to integrate our faith in all of life. Vos writes, "Undoubtedly the kingship of God, as his recognized and applied supremacy, is intended to pervade and control the whole human life in all its forms of existence.... These various forms of human life have each their own sphere in which they work and embody themselves." [78]

Vos points out that this is what the parable of the yeast teaches in Matthew 13:33. His biblical insights conclude that the main way to see the Kingdom of God, and thus look forward to its coming, is through the church and through Christians living holy lives in this changing culture. As the church ministers through word and sacrament, to draw and disciple people to Christ, and as Christians work to glorify God in all they do, the Kingdom of God becomes visible. As mentioned previously, from the parable of the hidden treasure and the pearl of great value, the discovery of the Kingdom produces a joy that becomes the engine of change. This is why Peter exhorts us to look forward to its coming and to hurry it along by holy and godly living. Vos would say that a significant part of what that looks like is participating in the gathering of the church, in word and sacrament, and to be sent out to glorify God in our vocations, families, recreation and in our neighborhoods. Vos is clear that this does not involve political power or control over society but rather a balance between spiritual growth and cultural engagement. Whenever God's divine power influences any sphere of human life with his Kingdom principles, we can begin to see the Kingdom of God. That may include such simple things as caring for the environment by recycling our plastics or loving our neighbors by involving ourselves in the more complex issues of sex trafficking or racial injustice. Whatever the sphere of human life it should involve developing people and places, not just serving them for their betterment. Author Bob Lupton says it this way, "Betterment does for others. Development enables others to do for themselves. Betterment improves conditions. Development strengthens capacity." [79]

The parable of the yeast affirms it is not by our power and control that the Kingdom of God comes. The Kingdom is a realm where Jesus exercises his power and control to glorify his Father and sustain his church, the body of Christ. That Kingdom is first and forever created, grown and sustained through the word of God, (parable of the sower). When the way of the Kingdom comes it is inclusive, (parable of the wheat and tares). It contains both good and bad, and we are called to co-exist until Christ's return. Only then in the final judgment, with the Kingdom fully established, will there be a separation. Therefore when we pray "Thy Kingdom come", we are also praying your word come and your way come. Yet in light of events globally and locally it is hard at times to see the Kingdom of God, to see Jesus exercising his power and control, especially if we are not looking forward to it and attempting to hurry it along.

The parable of the yeast is offered to encourage us and give us a confidence that the Kingdom is coming and is now here. The point of the parable is not so much about growth as it is about contrast. What starts out as a pinch of yeast in a huge batch of dough ends up present in all the bread. Once yeast is introduced permeation is inevitable. Jesus is teaching to his disciples and to his church, that we may seem insignificant compared to world events but eventually we will permeate the whole neighborhood and the whole world. We can have confidence that no matter how small our church, ministry, or even the gospel may seem it will become a nourishing loaf. The gospel may appear small compared to the cultural philosophies, political ideologies, and global economics of our day, but its effect is huge.

The apparent smallness of the coming Kingdom can sometimes scandalize. We are often ashamed of its size and are tempted to supplement the story to make it more attractive. We lack confidence in the coming Kingdom so we contrive contemporary realities of church, supported by unbiblical teaching. The bread is not rising fast enough so we manufacture and market our own replica. While it is a characteristic of yeast to be small it is also a characteristic for it to be alive and to permeate. The point and promise of the parable of the yeast is not that the whole world will be converted but that the little gospel has big effects. That bigness is not to be seen in a quantitative way as worldly bigness, but in a qualitative way as Kingdom bigness. The fruit of a good life and a mission-minded church provides loaves of bread for a needy world.

We've lost some of our confidence in God's coming Kingdom by trusting in the things of this world, reinforced by the materialistic false teaching of our culture and in some cases from the church itself. We end up with a plastic loaf of bread we make ourselves, that has no value, or we decide to give up baking all together because we believe we can't possibly nourish this opposing culture. Instead we settle for our own comfortable rules of holiness and building an acceptable version of a prosperity gospel. As C. S. Lewis has said, "Prosperity knits a man to the world. He feels that he is finding his place in it, while really it is finding its place in him."80 We end up doing what Peter told us not to do; we forget what God has done and has promised to do.

A high school orchestra can attempt to play Beethoven's Ninth symphony and the result may be far from perfect, maybe even awful. However, for some in the audience it may be their only encounter with Beethoven. As a church we may never come close to perfecting what the composer of the Kingdom had in mind but there is no other way for the music of the Kingdom to be heard on earth. This is why in Peter's concluding words he begins with, "while you are waiting for these things to happen, make every effort to live a pure and blameless life" (2 Peter 3:14).

"The way to Christian growth is often to allow oneself to be puzzled and startled by new apparent complexity ... Is it, after all, Jesus we want to discover and follow, or would we prefer an idol of our own making?" N. T. Wright, *The Challenge of Jesus* (InterVarsity Press, 1999).

CHAPTER 9 - GROWING CHRISTIANS FOR THE GLORY OF CHRIST

Do too many Christians just have faith in God because we need a source of comfort? In an interview for *Los Angeles Review of Books,* Hollywood screenwriter Dorothy Fortenberry attempted to address that question.

> The single most annoying thing [I hear about faith] …
> is the kind, patronizing way, that nonreligious people
> have of saying, "You know, sometimes I *wish* I were
> religious. I *wish* I could have that certainty. It just
> seems so *comforting* never to doubt things." Well,
> sometimes I wish I had the certainty of an atheist … I
> do not find religion to be comforting in the way that I
> think nonreligious people mean it …It is not comfort-
> ing to know quite as much as I do about how wea-
> selly and weak-willed I am when it comes to being as
> generous as Jesus demands. Thanks to church, I have
> a much stronger sense of the sort of person I would
> like to be, and I am forced to confront all the ways in
> which I fail, daily. Nothing promotes self-awareness
> like turning down an opportunity to bring children to
> visit their incarcerated parents. Or avoiding shifts at
> the food bank. Or calculating just how much I will
> put in the collection basket. Thanks to church, I have

looked deeply into my own heart and found it to be of
merely small-to-medium size. None of this is particularly comforting. [81]

The path of life is so full of traps and hurdles, it is not surprising
that some nonreligious people would imagine that faith could offer
some certainty and comfort in the midst of a chaotic world. Yet, while
Peter presents God's book as the answer to the traps and hurdles of
today's culture, many Christians prefer avoiding the Bible for some
of the very reasons Dorothy Fortenberry mentions. It is not always
particularly comfortable.

This perspective is consistent with Charles Taylor's diagnosis
of our challenging culture. Here is how James Smith summarizes
Taylor's point. "Our secular age is messier than many would lead us
to believe; that transcendence and immanence bleed into one another;
that faith is pretty much unthinkable, but abandonment to the abyss is
even more so." [82]

Too many false teachings and secular ideologies have led Christians
away from God to a comfortable individualized faith and yet our challenging culture has not completely abandoned the idea that a transcendent world exists. In the day-to-day realities of a sometimes hard
life, doubt mixes with devotion and faith blends with skepticism. We
are often more like a doubting Thomas than a fully devoted Christ
follower. Again, in his introduction to Taylor's *Secular Age*, Smith
writes, "Most of us live in this cross-pressured space, where both our
agnosticism and our devotion are mutually haunted and haunting. If
our only guides were the new atheists or religious fundamentalists,
we would never know this vast, contested terrain even existed, even
though most of us live in this space every day." [83]

This is the place, today's challenging culture, that God's sovereignty has created for His church to engage on our journey to a
kingdom holiness. It is not a place of comfort but of glorious trans-
formation. It is that uncomfortable space to bring the brokenness of

our self-glory to be crucified and healed, by glorifying Christ in our words and deeds. It is also quite possible that this cross-pressured space, this contested terrain, is a very similar context to which Peter was addressing in his second letter. The immanence, the reality, that Christ had not returned had bled into the transcendent idea of a final judgment, causing skepticism and even unbelief.

In his final verses of 2 Peter 3:14-18, the author instructs the readers to grow as Christians for the glory of Christ. Again, the false teaching around Christ's second coming had seduced the church into a comfortable faith and a promiscuous lifestyle. If Christ is not returning, let's party. Commentator Michael Green wrote, "'How will God find me?' is a searching question for Christians to ask, whether death or Christ's return be upper most in view." [84] Simply and more broadly put, how does the way we live reflect what we believe about God and the work of Christ?

Humanity loves to define and understand history based on how we have progressed and what we have accomplished. Therefore, we have classified periods of history, such as the Dark Ages, the Renaissance, the Enlightenment, the Industrial Age, and today the Internet Age. It is a man centered focus on the meaning of history. However, this final passage in second Peter gives us a God centered view of history: the age of salvation - the history of the world between the first and second coming of Christ. It is a history that is more important than the Renaissance of learning, the emergence of science or the rise of industry. It is a time that has opened the door to God, a time that has inaugurated his coming kingdom, a time where God is making all things new, a time of redemption and a time of salvation. The only history of eternal significance is the history of the church, carrying out God's mission, and the only biography of eternal significance is the lives of God's people, glorifying him in all they do.

Peter is telling us how to view this time we live in, how to think about God delaying Christ's return and to have God's perspective of this time in history. Those who believed that God's delay meant he either doesn't exist at all or he's uninvolved in the affairs of men, used the time for their own self-interest. Peter reinforces this by claiming Paul's letters have said the same thing. Paul writes in Romans 2:4, "Don't you realize how kind, tolerant, and patient God is with you? Or don't you care? Can't you see how kind he has been in giving you time to turn from your sin?" Peter is putting Paul's writings in the same category as his own, claiming an equal inspiration and authority while reaffirming that all Scripture is inspired by God and useful in teaching what is true. John Wesley once wrote, "Oh give me that book. At any price give me the book of God. Let me be homo unius libri (a man of one book)." [85] Oh that we in the church would be people of the book.

Peter goes on to admit that some of Paul's New Testament letters are hard to understand and consequently some people have taken God's word and forced it to mean something quite different than was intended. The mind of God is so much greater than our minds, so it is fair to say that there are parts of Scripture that seem too complex for our understanding. Yet to misunderstand Scripture is one thing but to twist it to make it say something untrue is something else. Peter says these people are ignorant and unstable. It is not that they don't know anything, it is that they refuse instruction and intentionally lead people away from the truth. Peter assures us, however, that their false teachings end in disaster for them. That's why James' Epistle tells us, "Not many of you should become teachers in the church, for those who teach will be judged with greater strictness" (James 3:1). This is not one of my favorite Scriptures.

Now while the issue of false teaching today may not be the denial of Christ's return, the application is still very relevant, especially coupled with a lazy faith and the prominence of individualism. Second Timothy 4:3 says, "The time is coming when people will no longer listen to right teaching. They will follow their own desires and will look for teachers who will tell them whatever they want to hear."

That time is here, and much of the church has become codependent with those who have itchy ears and will not put up with sound doctrine. Tell me what you want to hear and I can go to the internet to find seven ways to make you happy and pepper it with Scripture. The early church father Saint John Chrysostom wrote, "We must not mind insulting men, if by respecting them we offend God." [86] Maybe a good sermon should be the most demanding thing we hear all week. Yet in this individualistic, consumer oriented culture, it is hard to hold people's attention while not offending their sensibilities.

In his New York Times column, David Brooks discussed Mitch Albom's book, *The Five People You Meet in Heaven.* Brooks thinks we should fear Albom's "soft-core spirituality" and "easygoing narcissism." The eternal reward pictured in Albom's book is different than the biblical one. Brooks writes, "In this heaven, God and his glory are not the center of attention. It's all about you. Here, sins are not washed away. Instead, hurt is washed away. The language of good and evil is replaced by the language of trauma and recovery." [87]

As we have become seduced by a more individualized, comfortable Christian faith, we have also become less morally aware, less holy. The meaning of life has become whatever we want it to be, because after all it's our life. This is why Peter exhorts us to guard and grow our faith for the glory of Christ. Peter writes in 2 Peter 3:17-18, "I am warning you ahead of time, dear friends, so that you can watch out and not be carried away by the errors of these wicked people. I don't want you to lose your own secure footing. But grow in the special favor and knowledge of our Lord and Savior Jesus Christ."

Peter says watch out, be on guard, so you don't get carried away by the error of lawless people. He has referred to this error previously as cleverly invented stories, untruths that will tickle our ears and appeal to our individualism. We must guard our faith by being able to recognize these untruths. When I first graduated from college, my first real job was working in a bank. I was soon promoted to the head teller's position, which made me responsible for the cash in all the branches. That included being aware of counterfeit money. I was trained to know the intricate details of every denominational currency, from one dollar bills to hundred dollar bills. I was also made aware of how counterfeit money was made and what it looked and felt like. This is what Peter wants from us in order to grow as Christians, to know the details of biblical truth but to also be aware of the counterfeits being taught today.

Every week when we leave church we are entering into the mission field, a field where we encounter cleverly invented stories and world-views that will conflict with and attempt to seduce us away from our Christian view of life. It is hard, if not almost impossible, to be salt and light, to bring shalom to our work, our neighborhood, or even our family, if we don't know the truth, if we don't make our knowledge of Christian doctrine a high priority. We must know God's book so we can recognize falsehood.

We also must be aware of what God's moral expectations are so we can recognize lawlessness or wicked behavior. Lawlessness or wickedness is the vomit which dogs return to and the mud which pigs love to wallow in (2 Peter 2:22). Now, I know this seems like rather offensive language for our delicate tastes, but Peter is trying to make the point that the refusal to allow God to rule over our lives is lawlessness. If we find Peter's description a little repulsive, imagine how wicked behavior appears to God. All sin is lawlessness and wickedness to God, so Peter wants us to grow as Christians by not getting caught up in any false teaching that refuses to call sin, sin. A pig is going to wallow in the mud and putting lipstick on the pig doesn't change that reality.

Peter teaches us to grow our faith by recognizing error and knowing God's moral expectations, all so that we don't lose our secure footing. We must be alert to those who want to draw us away from the gospel's truth with a different teaching and a different moral expectation, no matter how attractive and comfortable it seems. It's a vivid picture of those who may offer a helping hand but make us wobble in our faith. The good news is that if we belong to Christ we may wobble but we will never fall from God's grace. Peter ends with a call to grow in that grace, the special favor and knowledge of our Lord and Savior Jesus Christ. Peter has used Lord and Savior throughout his letter. Lord speaks to Christ power to judge us and Savior reveals his willingness to save us on the day of judgment. We are to grow in that grace and knowledge.

Unfortunately, our sinful nature has a built in tendency to push Jesus to the back of our lives. Growing in grace is a frequent and deliberate effort to bring Jesus to the forefront of our lives. That is much of what Sunday worship helps us to do. Peter told us earlier that as Christians we have a responsibility to increase our knowledge of Christ. Here Peter, in essence, is saying it is impossible to standstill as a Christian, if our life is planted deeply in the word of God. Peter wants us to guard against being like a tree that does not grow, losing its stability in the earth and blown over by the winds of false teachings. On the other hand there is a tree which keeps its roots planted deeply in the grace of God's word, growing stable and strong, able to withstand the winds of false doctrine or the drought of a complacent faith.

Science writer Hope Jahren shares some interesting facts about plants, especially how a tiny seed starts to put down roots - the most essential thing for a plant's survival. She writes,

> No risk is more terrifying than that taken by the first root. A lucky root will eventually find water, but its first job is to anchor ... Once the first root is extended, the plant will never again enjoy any hope of relocating to a place less cold, less dry, less dangerous. Indeed, it will face frost, drought, and greedy jaws without any possibility of flight. [88]

She calls taking root a big "gamble," but if the seed takes root it can go down twelve, thirty, forty meters. The results are powerful. The tree's roots can "swell and split bedrock, and move gallons of water daily for years, much more efficiently than any pump yet invented by man." If the root takes root, then the plant becomes all but indestructible: "Tear apart everything aboveground—everything—and most plants can still grow rebelliously back from just one intact root. More than once. More than twice." [89]

Growing in God's grace is to anchor our spiritual roots in the water of God's word. Deep roots that can withstand the blowing cultural shifts that gradually move us into a comfortable Christianity that has lost its saltiness and dimmed our light. No matter how long we've been a Christian we cannot rest on the Sunday school lessons of our youth or even last month's sermon. We grow in grace by knowing more about Jesus but also by applying his promises through the power of his Holy Spirit in every sphere of life. Every person we meet, every place our feet tread, we bring Jesus to the front of our lives. We must choose to involve our Christian faith every moment and day of our lives.

Here is how J. I. Packer expresses this biblical understanding of "growing in grace" by quoting J. C. Ryle:

> When I speak of a man growing in grace, I mean simply this - that his sense of sin is becoming deeper, his faith stronger, his hope brighter, his love more extensive, his spiritual-mindedness more marked. He feels more of the power of godliness in his own heart. He manifests more of it in his life. He is going on from strength to strength, from faith to faith and from grace to grace. [90]

Orthodox church officials in Russia discovered in 2008 that one of their church buildings had disappeared. The 200 year old building north east of Moscow had gone unused for a decade but the orthodox church was experiencing growth and was considering reopening the church building. That's when they discovered their building wasn't there. They had to get to the bottom of this. After investigating the matter, the church officials did not blame aliens from outer space for the missing structure. Rather, they said the perpetrators were villagers from a nearby town, whom they said had taken and sold bricks from the building to a businessman. For each brick the thieves received one ruble, about four cents. This two-story church facility did not go from being a building to not being a building in one bulldozing stroke. Rather, the bricks were apparently chiseled out one by one by lots of people. [91]

In the same way, some churches, built not out of bricks but of "living stones" - that is of Christians - are not reduced in one fatal stroke but rather by Christians one by one choosing not to be involved. Not only staying home from church but choosing to do their own individual spiritual thing. Being "me" focused and becoming less morally aware, results in one less living stone. The church as God's display of Christ's glory and God's kingdom, is chiseled away, one living brick at a time.

As we stated in the introduction, Jesus asked his Father to not take us out of this world, even though we do not belong to this world. However, Jesus is praying for more than his disciples to be in the world, he is *sending* us into this world. Therefore, we are not to be of this world but we are to be *sent* into the world on God's mission. Lesslie Newbigin writes, "They are not to inhabit a ghetto, they are to go forth on a mission". [92] God's mission for his church is the continuation of Jesus' mission through the power of the Holy Spirit and "It is the Father's holiness which is the basis of the Son's mission." [93]

An uninvolved faith and false teaching feed each other, becoming a downward spiral and undermining our Lord's mission. Our lazy and complacent faith makes us susceptible to false doctrine and that untruth encourages our apathy. The only antidote to this deception is to grow our faith for the glory of Christ. We do that by embracing a kingdom holiness, through the trials of engaging our culture, with the truth of the gospel. The good news for this challenge is that God wrote a book just for that purpose.

EPILOGUE - ARE YOU THE MESSIAH OR SHOULD WE KEEP LOOKING?

2 Peter may be the least read book in the New Testament. Most of us don't like to hear negative things. While the author does offer us hope and calls us to remember afresh the gospel of grace, he hits the reader hard with the dangers of a complacent faith that makes one susceptible to the practices and false teachings of today. Our culture is rife with ideologies and irreligion that contradict the truth of Scripture. This pluralistic society offers many variations of truth in an attempt to make sense of reality. And we are too often eager to listen in order to spiritualize our selfish and lustful decisions - decisions that are driven by expectations of immediate gratification and self-fulfillment. When those expectations are not met we are left with disappointment and doubt in a God who we falsely believe is like our spiritual Santa Claus.

Historian Daniel Boorstin suggests that Americans suffer from an all-too-extravagant expectations. In his much quoted book, *The Image,* Boorstin makes the following observation about Americans expectations.

> We expect anything and everything. We expect the contradictory and the impossible. We expect compact cars to be spacious and luxury cars to be economical. We expect to be rich and charitable, powerful and merciful, kind and competitive. We expect to eat

whatever we want and stay thin, to go to the church of our choice and have our every need met. We expect to worship God and to be God. Never have a people expected so much more than life could offer and yet felt more deceived and disappointed. [94]

There was a man in Scripture who felt a similar mixture of deception and disappointment; a man who had certain expectations from the coming Messiah. His name was John the Baptist. Most of us know something about this man sent from God to give witness to the light coming into the world. We know he was a little strange, with his wardrobe of camel hair and his crazy diet of wild honey and locust wings, but he was admired for his integrity and obedience. Jesus said of John that among those born of women, there is no one greater. John enjoyed two unique privileges. First he was one of Jesus' cousins; they probably spent much time together growing up. Second, he had this calling to prepare the way for Jesus, announcing the arrival of Jesus' ministry. He boldly directed people to Jesus, proclaiming, "Behold the Lamb of God who takes away the sins of the world" (John 1:29). John lived his entire adult life pointing people to Jesus. When Jesus arrived on the scene, those who had been following John started going to Jesus' meetings but John told his concerned disciples, "I must decrease and Jesus must increase" (John 3:30). John was full of hope and expectations, however, a year later John's circumstances changed.

In his zeal for holiness, John challenged one of history's most powerful leaders, Herod Antipas, about an affair he was having with his brother's wife. Herod didn't take kindly to being called an adulterer, a sinner, so he threw John into prison. It is worth noting that Jesus taught his followers to challenge their fellow believers who sin and to forgive them if they repent. However, that act is not always well received and can end with our brother or sister walking away, refusing to talk to us, and putting us into a kind of spiritual prison of unforgiveness.

It is from a literal prison, however, that John sends a message to Jesus: "Are you the Messiah or should we keep looking" (Matthew 11:3). It's a surprising question coming from John the Baptist. This is the one who said of Jesus, "I am not worthy to untie the straps of his sandals" (John 1:27), and now John wants to know if Jesus is the One.

We need to understand John's pain here. He had pointed thousands of people to Jesus, he had given his life to that mission and now he was wondering if he was wrong. Had he actually lead people astray? What had caused John to be so disappointed in Jesus? John knew Jesus was giving sight to the blind, healing the sick, raising the dead and preaching to the poor. What bothers John was what Jesus was not doing. Jesus was not fulfilling John's expectations, and according to pastor and professor Darrell Johnson, he was not fulfilling them on two levels. [95]

Disappointment comes when Jesus doesn't fill our theological expectations. When he doesn't act in a way we think God should behave. John's preaching summarized his expectations (John 3:15-17). John believed that Jesus would baptize with the Holy Spirit and with fire. These expectations are also promises from the Old Testament prophets concerning the coming Messiah. He would pour out his Holy Spirit on all of his followers and he would bring fire to judge his enemies. Fire is a symbol of God's judgment and John's expectations were that when the Messiah comes he will destroy all evil and purge the world of sin. The Messiah would come and baptize the righteous with the Holy Spirit and baptize the wicked with fire. He would baptize the good guys and burn up the bad guys. So in other words, turn or burn. This action would come all at once and that is why John warned people to be ready to repent and be baptized. The Messiah is coming to separate the wheat from the chaff and to burn up the chaff.

Instead Jesus was hanging out with the chaff, the wicked, the unrighteous, the bad guys. Now, thank God that was true because it is also a picture of you and me. At one time we were the chaff, the un-righteous, but Jesus came and hung out with us to save us from the fire. However, this didn't fit into John's theological expectations, so he had to ask are you the Messiah or should we keep looking. Yet John's question was not just theological, it was also personal.

Disappointment also comes when Jesus doesn't fill our personal expectations. John's question arises out of his personal experience, his disappointment had another level. He was lying in a cold hard prison cell, imprisoned by the kind of person Jesus was supposed to destroy. Herod was upstairs getting drunk and having an affair and Jesus is out having a feast with prostitutes, tax collectors and all kind of sinners, while John sits in prison. No wonder he's disappointed and maybe even feels a little deceived. John has to be thinking, if you are the Messiah, the King, the Lord of life, why am I sitting in prison and why are you not doing anything about it?

Below the surface of most theological questions and controver-sies, lies a deep emotional wound or disappointment. We affirm the sovereignty of God, the Lordship of Christ and we see some evidence of God's reign in our world. Then our personal experiences seem to tell us God is not always in charge. Our personal expectations are not being met. Where is our all powerful God in this world of terror-ism, where is our reconciling Christ in this nation's divisive political ideology and where is the shalom of the Holy Spirit in this country's racial tension? Where was God's healing touch for our loved ones who died? It is the age old question of why do the wicked prosper and the righteous suffer? Of course the simple answer is sin, the broken-ness of the world we live in. Life does not always work the way our American culture has taught us to expect.

Too many of us Christians have compartmentalized our lives apart from our faith. Politics, family, jobs, recreation, and relationships, all good things, get put on a par or even higher than God. Our faith is not fully integrated into every area of our life. Jesus is not Lord over ev-ery activity and every relationship, setting us up for disappointments in both our theological and personal expectations. Tim Keller writes, "Sin is building your life and meaning on anything, even very good things, more than on God." [96]

In the Spring of 2004, our son-in-law and my assistant pastor was diagnosed with an aggressive form of colon cancer. Our family, friends, church and the greater Christian community, surrounded our daughter and three young children with love and support, and fervently prayed for her husband's healing. That healing, we all expected, never came. Our son-in-law, at age 33, went to be with our Heavenly Father in January of 2005. My wife and I quickly jumped into the task of ministering to the needs and grief of our daughter and grandchildren, as well as our church family. Not only did our church have hope and expectations for healing, but they believed at some point in the future our son-in-law would take over for me as their lead pastor. All of our personal expectations were dashed, and as it seemed to us, God was not who he was supposed to be.

In the busyness of caring for others, it took me months to realize the connection between my personal and theological disappointments with God. I was deeply wounded by God's apparent unwillingness to heal. There was never a more obvious opportunity for God's miraculous intervention. Here was a man who loved Jesus, his family and our neighborhood. He turned down an opportunity to become the senior pastor at a much larger church to come and serve in a poor urban church and community, working for his father-in-law. In addition to that, our whole family had lived and ministered in the inner city since our children were very young. Suddenly there it was. I had unknowingly succumbed to a false theological principle. Since my family and I were sacrificing so much for God, nothing too traumatic would ever happen to us. Yes, we would struggle, make less money, endure the trials of urban life and ministry, but at the end of the day God would at least preserve our lives. A works righteousness had just been revealed. I preached and taught a salvation by grace alone through faith alone in Christ alone. Yet in the deep recesses of my heart was hidden a theological and personal expectation that I could be good enough so that God would keep the worst from ever happening to me or my family. I had made the very good thing of ministry in the inner city equal with God himself. Jesus was not fully Lord over all my life and ministry.

I have always recognized that this Christian life is a journey of peaks and valleys, of joys and disappointments, lived out in the body of Christ, the church, accompanied by the presence of God's Holy Spirit. It is also a journey that must tolerate the tares in our lives, the weeds in our garden, that contribute to our disappointments (Matthew 13:24-30). There will always be people and circumstances that reject us, hurt us, let us down and even sin against us. Even though the enemy has sowed the weeds, Jesus instructs us to leave them alone and not try to root them out, or figure them out, because we might harm the good in the process of trying to pull out the bad. It's not that Jesus is indifferent to the weeds in our lives but he promises they will be dealt with in the final judgment. He is teaching that we are to coexist with the good and the bad, the joys and the tragedies. Dale Bruner quotes Augustine,

> There are within the church both good and bad, as I
> often express it, wheat and chaff. Let no one leave the
> floor before the time, let him bear with the chaff in
> the time of threshing, let him bear with it in the floor.
> For in the barn he will have none of it to bear with...
> In heart be always separated from the bad, in body be
> united with them for a time, only with caution. [97]

This parable guards us against hunkering down in our theological or ideological communities. It also should begin to dismantle our dualistic worldview that separates the sacred and the secular, rather than integrating our faith in all of life. The weeds in our lives are inevitable, whether it is difficult people or painful tragedies, and the sorting out process is in the hands of God.

That is why Jesus says, "God blesses those who do not fall away because of me" (Matthew 11:6). In other words, Jesus is saying I know you are disappointed in the way I am doing things but trust me. I am asking you to tolerate the terrible tares in your life. Engage with those on the other side of the ideological aisle, love that annoying neighbor next door, pray for the terrorists around the world, and trust me with the unexpected death of your loved one.

Even if Jesus had struck Herod with fire, freed John the Baptist from prison, and pulled up the other tares in John's life, he would never have been free from disappointments apart from a deep trusting relationship with Jesus. We may think we are stumbling or offended over the people and the trials in our lives but we are really stumbling and offended over Jesus because he is moving too slowly or not removing the hardships in our lives. The resulting temptation is to then look for someone else, to walk away, or to find a false messiah. However, Jesus assures us, he is the promised One. Jesus is saying, let me be who I am, in my way, in my time, and blessed is the one who is not offended by me.

This was the issue Peter is addressing in his second letter. It had been three decades since Christ had been crucified and resurrected but nothing had improved or even changed. They had expected to see Christ's return or at least a change in the status quo. Was Jesus really who he said he was? If Jesus is not coming back let's consider some alternatives to make sense of our present reality, like indulging in the pleasures of life that only money can bring. The false teachers were instructing them to do just that, enabling them to "deliberately" forget the truth about God. Their lackadaisical lifestyle was being supported by a defective doctrine, giving them a place of comfort, a religious appearance, but without the holiness of God's coming Kingdom.

Many in the church live in that same place today. The challenging culture has taught us to doubt or even reject so much of God's truth, as revealed in Scripture. In our fear of being seen as too holy, we find a comfortable and acceptable level of obedience to those around us, a place where we are not ostracized by the culture and are still received by Christians. Our standard for holiness is a minimal obedience inside the church and the best of living a "good life" outside the Christian faith. However, the true standard for holiness is no less than being conformed to the character of Christ and living out that holiness in all of life.

This kingdom holiness, this higher level of obedience to our King, is what enables the church to help usher in God's kingdom and to transform our challenging culture. As citizens of this kingdom our holiness is not to be seen as a prideful status but rather as a humble servant who confidently serves and participates in the broader culture for the common good. Our holy condition, from beginning to end, is only by God's grace.

Our strongest temptation, however, is conform to this world. The prefix con means "with" and we prefer to be "with it." We long to fit in and our culture pressures us to conform to its patterns, to the accepted public facts of the plausibility structure. But the Apostle Paul says we are to be transformed and the prefix trans means to be "above and beyond." A kingdom holiness calls us to live above and beyond the standards of this challenging culture. We are called to a higher level of obedience, a more excellent way of life.

Once again as Peter writes in his final words, "You already know these things, dear friends. So be on guard; then you will not be carried away..." by the false teaching of our culture. "Rather, you must grow in the grace and knowledge of our Lord and Savior Jesus Christ" (2 Peter 3:17-18).

SMALL GROUP DISCUSSION QUESTIONS

Introduction

1. How well do you balance "being in the world but not of the world"? What is your biggest challenge of being too much of the world?

2. What does the author mean by the term "kingdom holiness"? In this challenging culture, what distinguishes you as a citizen of God's kingdom?

3. Identify some "protective buffers" that may be keeping you from living a holy life. What are some "hard realities" in your life that have put you in tune with what God was doing, causing your growth as a Christian?

4. Michael frost asks, "What if we looked at the churches mission as empowering followers of Christ to infiltrate all the domains of society as agents of the mission of God". What are those various domains in your life? What would it look like two infiltrate them?

5. The author suggests "pragmatism has caused many Christians to concede the dialogue over truth to the prevailing culture.... becoming more comfortable with what works over affirming the truth". Over what issues, and why, have you conceded the dialogue to the culture?

Chapter 1

1. How well do you listen to warnings? What factors determines how serious you would take the warning?

2. How do you know if the power of Christ is giving you everything you need to live a holy life? What can you do if there is no evidence of a holy life?

3. What is this power of Christ and how do we increase our access to this power?

4. What keeps you from accessing Christ's divine power to live a godly life?

5. How might God be asking you to re-order your life in order to live a more holy life?

Chapter 2

1. Have you ever made an irrevocable promise? What was it?

2. Explain the two general categories of God's promises.

3. Give some examples, from childhood, changes, or crisis in your life, where you felt God's promises were insufficient for what you were experiencing.

4. What are some worldly things or ideas you trust in for your security over the promises of God and why?

5. Why is it all right to see the promises of God as a crutch?

Chapter 3

1. What is meant by the term R.O. I.? How have you found yourself applying it in the context of ministry or relationships?

2. Explain the extremes of legalism (law) and libertinism (grace). What are the consequences of leaning too far either way?

3. What does Peter mean when he says, "make every effort to apply the benefits"?

4. The author suggests we make every effort.... when we make it a priority, measure our progress, and maintain our perspective. What might that look like in your life?

5. What are the promises that come with making every effort?

Chapter 4

1. What determines how well you respond to authority?

2. In what areas of your life do you give God's Word the most authority and why? In what areas do you give it the least authority and why?

3. What is meant by the inspiration of Scripture? What are two important conclusions we can make from that inspiration?

4. What scriptures, if any, have you chosen, or been tempted to choose, as no longer relevant for our culture today and why?

5. Diogenes Allen tells us the Latin root of authority means "that which allows growth and life". Thus the author states God's authority in Scripture is a precondition for our relationship with Him. How do you respond to that statement?

Chapter 5

1. What are some areas in your Christian life where you have settled for good enough instead of striving for well done?

2. What are some ways that Peter suggests we can recognize false teaching? Where have you seen some false teaching that was imported from the culture?

3. Why is it hard to stand for the truth when it goes against what is popular and plausible?

4. How do you defend Christianity when it is seen as narrow and exclusive?

5. If we are saved for eternity, why does it matter whether we strive to live a holy life?

Chapter 6

1. Where have you found yourself seeking a more comfortable and homogeneous life? How might it have made you more susceptible to false teaching?

2. How have you shown favoritism that may have contributed to the exclusion of outsiders?

3. Peter says the character of false teachers involve greed, sensuality, and arrogance. What does he say are the consequences for both unbelievers and believers?

4. If individualism is the idol that we worship and marketing is the gospel that enhances our image, how then is our work a form of salvation?

5. The author states that our identity and power can come by the measurement of our differences from others. What standards do you use to evaluate others different than you?

Chapter 7

1. How do you most often handle pressure and stress?

2. How can stirring up pure thoughts help us overcome the pressures of life?

3. Chesterton wrote, "We do not want .... a church that will move with the world. We want a church that moves the world". What does the church need to change to move the world? What do you need to do?

4. In your lifetime how have you seen God at work that has changed our world?

5. Even though we don't always know exactly what God is doing in our lives, or the world, how do you maintain hope that God is an ever holy and loving presence?

Chapter 8

1. Regardless of your theological view, what honest emotions arise in you when a discussion of end times comes up?

2. How does Peter suggest we as Christians can hurry along Christ's coming and the end of this world?

3. Peter has more than once mentioned his readers willful forgetfulness about some things of God. What are some aspects of Scripture that you intentionally forget or would like to forget?

4. How do you feel about God destroying the unrepentant or unbeliever? How would you respond to those who see God as arbitrary or unfair, deciding who is in and who is not?

5. According to the teaching of the parables in Matthew 13 how does the Kingdom of God become visible? How do these parables of the Kingdom offer you hope?

Chapter 9

1. How has your faith in Christ provided you comfort amidst the traps and hurdles of this life? When has your Christian life not been particularly comfortable?

2. When has doubt in Christ overcome your devotion to Christ? How did you overcome the doubt?

3. What does Peter mean when he instructs us to grow in God's grace for the glory of Christ? How do you attempt to do that?

4. How have you at times pushed Jesus to the back of your life and how do you bring Him back to the forefront of your life?

5. Jesus doesn't want to take us out of this world, even though we don't belong to it, but rather send us into the world on God's mission. Where specifically is your mission field each week?

Epilogue

1. What were some of your greatest expectations that resulted in disappointments and doubts in God?

2. What are some alternatives to Christ you may have considered in order to make sense of the disappointments and chaos of life?

3. What are some good things that you made, or were tempted to make, as an ultimate thing, as an idol?

4. How have you found yourself conforming to the world in order to fit in and not be seen as too holy?

5. What are the challenges in a Kingdom Holiness to live above and beyond the standards of our culture?

END NOTES

[1] I am using "kingdom holiness" similar to "holy worldliness" used by Dr. Alec Vidler, *Essays in Liberality*, (London, S.C.M. Press, 1957).

[2] J. I. Packer, *We Can Overcome*, Christianity Today. (10-02-00).

[3] George Barna, *Growing True Disciples*, (Colorado Springs, CO: Waterbook Press, 2001), 48.

[4] Doug Hall, *The Cat and the Toaster*, (Eugene, OR: Wilfred and Stock, 2010), 14.

[5] This idea is from Henry Nouwen's story as a chaplain on a cruise ship where he was told to stay out of the way while the ship was finding its way through a thick fog but then the captain decided that this might be the only time Nouwen was really needed. Henri Nouwen, *The Wounded Healer*, (Garden City: Image/Doubleday, 1979), 87.

[6] Rodney Clapp, *A Peculiar People: The Church as Culture in a Post-Christian Society*, (Downers Grove: InterVarsity Press, 1996) 20.

[7] Ibid. 20.

[8] Ibid. 211.

[9] Ibid. Part of Clapp quotes Michael Warren, "Imitating Jesus in a Time of Imitation" in *Schooling Christians*, ed. Stanley Hauerwas and John H. Westerhoff (Grand Rapids: Eerdmans, 1992), 254.

[10] Joseph Stowell, "Preaching for Change", *The Big Idea of Biblical Preaching*, ed. Keith Willhite and Scott Gibson, (Grand Rapids: Baker Books, 1999), 138.

[11] Eugene Peterson, A Generous Savior, (The Gathering, 2012), 32.

[12] Clapp, *A Peculiar People,* 190.

[13] David Goetz, "Suburban Spirituality" posted June 2003 at www. christianity.com/ct/2003/007, 4.

[14] Goetz, "Suburban Spirituality", 7.

[15] Ibid.

[16] Amy Sherman, *Restorers of Hope,* (Wheaton, IL: Crossway Books, 1997), 230.

[17] Tim Keller, *Center Church,* (Grand Rapids, MI: Zondervan, 2012), 182.

[18] Lesslie Newbigin, "Can The West Be Converted", *International Bulletin of Missionary Research,* 11(1), Jan. 1987. pp. 2-7.

[19] Ibid.

[20] Ibid.

[21] Ibid.

[22] Ibid.

[23] Ibid.

[24] Michael Frost, *Incarnate,* (Downers Grove, IL: InterVarsity Press, 2014). 140.

[25] Fredrick Dale Bruner, *Matthew, A Commentary, Vol. 2* (Dallas, TX: Word Publishing, 1990), 511. My understanding of these parables is credited to Bruner's commentary on Mathew.

[26] James K. A. Smith, *How (Not) To Be Secular,* (Grand Rapids, MI: Eerdmans, 2014). vii.

[27] Ibid.

[28] G. K. Chesterton. While sourceless this quote has been readily attributed to Chesterton.

[29] C. S. Lewis, *God in the Dock,* (Grand Rapids, MI: Eerdmans, 1970). 59.

[30] Jerry Bridges, *Pursuit of Holiness* (Carol Stream, IL: Tyndale House, 2006).

[31] Douglas Moo, *The NIV Application Commentary, 2 Peter, Jude,* (Grand Rapids, MI: Zondervan, 1996). 41.

[32] John Calvin, *Institutes of the Christian Religion,* (Peabody, MA: k, 2008). 142-143.

[33] I paraphrased this from Douglas Groothuis, *Creeds, Slogans, and Full-orbed Orthodoxy,* (Radix, Fall 1985). Christianity Today, Vol. 30, no.8.

[34] Quoted in The Gathering, *David Brooks: A Holy Friend,* (10-2-14).

[35] Credit for these two categories to Lucas and Christopher Green, *The Message of 2 Peter & Jude,* (Downers Grove IL: InterVarsity, 1995). 51-53.

[36] Maxwell Maltz, *Psycho-Cybernetics,* (New York, NY: Simon and Schuster, 1960)

[37] Lucas and Green, *The Message of 2 Peter & Jude,* 57.

[38] J. N. D. Kelly, *A Commentary on the Epistles Peter and Jude,* (London: A. and C. Black, 1969; Peabody: Hendrikson, 1988). 307.

[39] Mark Galli, former editor of Christian History, now managing editor of Christianity Today; source: 131 Christians You Should Know (Broadman & Holman, forthcoming).

[40] Sam Shoemaker, in a July 1955 speech commemorating the 20th anniversary of the founding of Alcoholics Anonymous.

[41] Charles Piller, *Divine Inspiration from the Masses,* LA Times, (7-23-06).

[42] Kathy Schiffer, *A Bible and a Gun: The History of the Pony Express,* (National Catholic Register: Blog, 4/3/2017.

[43] D. M. Lloyd Jones, *Expository Sermons on 2 Peter,* (Edinburgh: The Banner of Truth Trust, 1999). 99.

[44] Quoted on Larry King Now, *"The State of Faith in America"* (8-20-14).

[45] Tim Keller, in the sermon *Literalism: Isn't the Bible Historically Unreliable and Regressive?,* PreachingToday.com

[46] Diogenes Allen in Quest: *The Search for Meaning through Christ.* Christianity Today, Vol. 40, no. 7.

[47] D. M. Lloyd Jones, *Expository Sermons on 2 Peter,* 100.

[48] Salena Zito, *Needed: Leaders With Moral Compasses,* Tribune Review, 5/16/2015.

[49] John Calvin, *Hebrews; 1and 2 Peter, Calvin's New Testament Commentaries, Vol. 12* (Grand Rapids: Eerdmans, 1989). 345.

[50] Lydia Saad, *Record Few Americans Believe Bible Is Literal Word of God*, news.gallup.com, Social & Policy Issues, (05/05/17).

[51] Neal Donald Walsch, *Conversations With God*, (New York, Berkeley: 1996). 3.

[52] Elizabeth Gilbert, *Eat, Pray, Love*, (New York, Riverhead Books: 2006).

[53] Alice in Wonderland (Walt Disney, 1951), rated G, directed by Hamilton Luske and Clyde Geronimi.

[54] Adapted from Brenda Salter McNeil, Roadmap to Reconciliation (InterVarsity Press, 2015). 22-23.

[55] Carol Kuruvilla, *Researchers Discover Common Thread Among Christians Who Voted for Trump*, (www.huffingtonpost.com, 4/14/18). 2-3.

[56] Tim Keller, *Every Good Endeavor*, (New York, N.Y., Penquin Group, 2012). 132.

[57] *Frederick Dale Bruner*, Matthew, A Commentary, Vol. 1 (Dallas, TX: Word Publishing, 1990), 299-307. My insights are credited to Bruner's commentary on Mathew.

[58] Oliver Stone, Movie *Wall Street*, (New York, NY: American Entertainment Partners, 1987).

[59] Edith Zimmerman, *99 Ways to Be Naughty in Kazakhstan*, The New York Times (8-5-12).

[60] Nicholas Wolterstorff, J*ustice: Rights and Wrongs*,(Princeton, NJ: Princeton University Press, 2008).

[61] Volf, Miroslav, *Exclusion and Embrace, A Theological Exploration of Identity, Otherness and Reconciliation*. (Nashville, TN: Abingdon Press, 1996). 28.

[62] Ibid.

[63] On seeing anti-black graffiti in Tennessee, 1970 (Attributed by Bill Moyers).

[64] Lewis Smedes, "The Journey to Integrity," Preaching Today, Tape No. 61.

[65] G. K. Chesterton, *Issues and G. K.'s Answers*, Christianity Today (07-01-02)

[66] David Wells, *No Place for Truth, or, Whatever Happened to Evangelical Theology?* Christianity Today, Vol. 38, no. 8.

[67] Larry Hurtado, *Why Did Anyone Become a Christian in the First Three Centuries?* (Milwaukee, WI, Marquette University Press, 2016). This is my summary of Hurtado's thoughts.

[68] Haddon Robinson, "How Does God Keep His Promises?," Preaching Today, Tape No. 130.

[69] Comes from an OmniPoll conducted in an online study of 1,066 U.S. adults in July of 2015. Barna defines "biblical worldview" as believing that absolute moral truth exists; the Bible is totally accurate in all of the principles it teaches; Satan is considered to be a real being or force, not merely symbolic; a person cannot earn their way into Heaven by trying to be good or do good works; Jesus Christ lived a sinless life on earth; and God is the all-knowing, all-powerful creator of the world who still rules the universe today.

[70] Ibid.

[71] D. M. Lloyd Jones, *Expository Sermons on 2 Peter*, 174.

[72] Frederick Buechner, *Wishful Thinking: A Seekers ABC* (New York, NY: Harper Collins, 1993), 58.

[73] Lucas and Green, *The Message of 2 Peter & Jude*, 145.

[74] Henri Nouwen, *The Wounded Healer*, (New York, N.Y.: Image Books Doubleday, 1979), 5-6.

[75] Jim Holt, *"Eternity for Atheists,"* The New York Times Magazine (7-29-07) and The Barna Group, 2002.

[76] D. M. Lloyd Jones, *Expository Sermons on 2 Peter*, 197.

[77] Geerhardus Vos, *The Teaching of Jesus Concerning the Kingdom of God and the Church,* (Eugene, Ore. Wipt & Stock, 1998), 162-163.

[78] Ibid.

[79] Robert Lupton, *And You Call Yourself a Christian*, (Chicago, IL: CCDA Institute, 2004), 35.

[80] C. S. Lewis, *The Screwtape Letters* (New York N.Y.: Macmillan, 1961), 132.

[81] Dorothy Fortenberry, *"Half-Full of Grace,"* Los Angeles Review of Books (6-8-17).

[82] James K. A. Smith, *How (Not) To Be Secular*, x.

[83] Ibid. 4.

[84] Michael Green, *The Second Epistle General of Peter and the General Epistle of Jude*, (Grand Rapids, MI: Eerdmans, 1968) 143.

[85] John Wesley, *The Works of the Rev. John Wesley* (New York: J. & J. Harper, 1826) 5.

[86] Saint John Chrysostom, *Six Books on the Priesthood*. (Graham Neville: St. Vladimir's Press, 1977) 65.

[87] David Brooks, *Hooked on Heaven Lite*, www.NYTimes.com, (3-9-04).

[88] Quoted and adapted from Hope Jahren, *Lab Girl* (New York, NY: Knopf, 2016), 45-46.

[89] Ibid.

[90] J. I. Packer, *Rediscovering Holiness*. (Ann Arbor, MI: Vine Books, 1992), 161.

[91] Craig Brian Larson, editor of PreachingToday.com; source: "Russian Orthodox Church Stolen Brick by Brick," Associated Press, (11-13-08).

[92] Lesslie Newbigin, *The Light Has Come*, (Grand Rapids, MI: Eerdmans, 1982), 231.

[93] Bruce Milne, *The Message of John*, (Downers Grove, IL: Inter-Varsity Press, 1993), 246.

[94] Daniel Boorstin, *The Image*, (New York, NY: Macmillan, 1987), Introduction.

[95] Darrell Johnson, *For Those Who Are Disappointed*, (www. PreachingTodaySermons.com, tape #51). I used Johnson's two points that disappointments come from theological and personal expectations but exposited from my own insights and from Frederick Dale Bruner, *Matthew, A Commentary, Vol. 1* (Dallas, TX: Word Publishing, 1990) 408-413.

[96] Tim Keller, *The Reason for God*, (New York, NY: Dutton, 2008), 275.

[97] Frederick Dale Bruner, *Matthew, A Commentary, Volume 2*, 497.

9 781633 572027